From Police Headquarters

From Police Headquarters

True Tales from the Big City Crime Beat

JOCKO THOMAS

Stoddart

Published by
Stoddart Publishing Co. Limited
34 Lesmill Road
Toronto, Canada
M3B 2T6

CANADIAN CATALOGUING IN PUBLICATION DATA

Thomas, Jocko
    From police headquarters

ISBN 0-7737-2419-2

1. Thomas, Jocko. 2. Criminals - Ontario - Toronto - History - 20th century. 3. Crime - Ontario - Toronto - History - 20th century. 4. Crime and the press - Ontario - Toronto. 5. Reporters and reporting - Ontario - Toronto - Biography. 6. Journalists - Ontario - Toronto - Biography. I. Title.

PN4914.C74T48 1990 070.4'49364'092
C90-094399-8CONTENTS

Indexing: Heather L. Ebbs
Typesetting: Tony Gordon Ltd.
Printed in Canada

For Marj, Judge Ron, David and Leslie

From Police Headquarters

Contents

Prologue: Impolite History   *1*

1. In Which the Author Begins Sixty Years of Crime   *4*
2. My First Scoop   *10*
3. My Innocence Wanes   *16*
4. The Night Police Beat   *22*
5. Labatt Blues   *28*
6. Draper   *33*
7. Red Ryan   *40*
8. Thousands Thought an Innocent Man Was Hanged   *45*
9. City of Bookies   *50*
10. The Murder of Jimmy Windsor   *57*
11. Scooped by the Censors   *64*
12. Making the News in Cobourg   *72*
13. The Triple Hanging   *82*
14. How My Hustle for a Scoop Almost Landed Me in Jail   *87*
15. Getting Away with Murder   *100*
16. The Long, Slow Death of Stanley Buckowski   *110*
17. The Boyd Gang Saga   *121*
18. The Day I Met Igor Gouzenko   *134*
19. The Blood of Marion McDowell   *142*
20. The Case of the Missing Bridge   *149*
21. The Plot to Kidnap Marilyn Bell   *156*
22. The Death of John Chisholm   *164*

23. Well-organized Crime   *174*

24. Justice   *181*

25. The Big Fix   *190*

26. The Politics of Policing   *196*

27. Dead Children   *204*

28. So Long   *211*

Index   214

Prologue:
Impolite History

THE SKIES CLEARED over Fort Frances, a town in northwestern Ontario, and the temperature plunged well below zero that March night in 1945. I shivered outside the small jailhouse as I waited for the official notice to be posted, affirming that the legal hanging of three men had been carried out for an atrocious crime I had labeled the Hot Stove murder case. Three men did die that night, on a scaffold the hangman had built himself, and I was there to report the drama of the occasion for the *Toronto Star*.

The three men and one other had been convicted for the unbelievably cruel torture and subsequent death of a woman they had stretched out on a hot kitchen stove to make her tell where she had hidden her money. She had only $700, which they didn't get. In his confession, one of the men said he had been led to believe they would get $20,000 — "and I never seen $200 in my life." For the man who escaped the noose, the reward for helping the police solve the crime was life in prison.

Newspaper reporters in Canada don't see hangings now, but they did up until the 1930s, as official witnesses. However, reporters continued to witness executions in American prisons, and seven years after the Fort Frances hangings, I didn't have to wait for any notice to confirm that a Toronto man had died in the gas chamber at San Quentin. In a sensational Death Row interview with him seven months earlier, he had confessed to murdering three people in Toronto and an old woman in Los Angeles. I was outside the chamber, looking in through the glass, as the cyanide slowly choked him to death.

These weren't the only execution stories I wrote over the six decades I covered crime for the *Star*. I was an unofficial visitor when a man was hanged in Kingston for killing a prison guard. And I remember a rough night at the hands of the provincial police in 1946, when I tried to ask the hangman some questions about his execution that day of a husband and wife in the Welland jail.

One evening in 1952, two Toronto detectives had a steak dinner at my home. Days later, I had to write the story of how one had been mortally wounded and the other badly shot up on College Street by two members of the notorious Boyd Gang. Seven years after that, I had to put my personal feelings aside and write about the High Park suicide of a man who had been one of the city's greatest detectives and certainly the best chief of police it had ever known.

Those are but a few of the grim memories I have of my time as a police reporter after beginning my career as a six-dollar-a-week copy boy at the *Star* in 1929. I covered the police beat in Toronto during the Great Depression, when a ten-dollar candy store holdup made news, right through the razzle-dazzle days of Toronto journalism, when the *Star* and the *Evening Telegram*, later known as the *Telegram*, were locked in an all-out war to the death for circulation. That was in the late forties, the fifties and early sixties, when the scoop was still king and a reporter would do almost anything to get one.

Newspaper work has since changed. The excitement of the next deadline is gone and the bitter rivalry between reporters is only a memory. Today there are almost as many female reporters as there are males. And reporters now come from journalism schools, rather than from the mob of young men clustered around the copy boys' bench. Shouts of "boy" to summon someone to rush copy from the typewriter to the city desk no longer fill the newsrooms, and today the writing is done on word processors. In my retirement now, I have to drive around looking for places that still sell ribbons for my old Underwood.

I'm sure that the young people in the profession today find it just as thrilling and rewarding as I did when I was their age, but I wouldn't have missed my time for the world. The city was much smaller, of course, though that didn't make much difference when it came to murder, which was just as brutal and final then as it is today. But it also seemed a much more innocent, less frenzied place, when one crime beat reporter who was willing to put in the hours could be reasonably sure he knew most of the cops and the rounders and pretty well had a line on all the latest excitement. In my time, I believe I recorded a good portion of Toronto's unofficial history, the eccentric and often nasty underside of city life that the polite historians ignore. And, as I've said, I would not have missed it for anything.

But the odd thing is, I nearly did miss it. When I joined the *Star* as a copy boy in 1929, being a reporter was the farthest thing from my mind. I was there to become a printer. Now, nearly sixty years later, I can still remember almost the exact moment I realized I would much rather chase the news than print it.

1

In Which the Author Begins Sixty Years of Crime

IT WAS DURING the 1930 marathon swim at the Canadian National Exhibition on Toronto's waterfront. The group picture taken outside the press tent is one of my most prized possessions and a poignant recall of the day that changed my life.

The big swim had been an annual feature at the CNE since 1928, the year after seventeen-year-old George Young of Toronto had driven his motorcycle to California and won $25,000 from the Wrigley chewing gum company by beating hundreds of swimmers in the Catalina Island marathon to decide the world's champion distance swimmer.

Elwood Hughes, the CNE's sports director, decided that Young's participation in the swim would be the biggest drawing card ever. Those were summer days when the Toronto dailies sold stacks of newspapers on the CNE grounds and aggressively competed to have the very latest sports results in their final editions, which didn't go to press until six in the evening.

I had been picked to cover the lap timer's location on the seawall. Lou Marsh, the sports editor, and his assistant, Alexandrine Gibb, drove me across the waterfront to the spot. My job was to get the time each swimmer took to complete a lap and rush it down to a telegraph operator, who sent it to the *Star*. The task gave me the delicious feeling that I was part of a large team of *Star* people covering an important event, although all I had to "report" was a column of lap times.

Young was the favorite, but he gave up early and didn't finish. When the race was over and the reporters had sent in their overnight stories by telephone from the press tent, the bar was opened. Those were the days of hard-drinking newsmen, many of whom were itinerant, and so unreliable in turning up for work that the *Star* paid them by voucher only for the days they were actually on the job.

At seventeen, I wasn't legally old enough to drink, but I had had many a drink before, mostly at Christmas. In the press tent, a couple of Tom Collinses were shoved my way by the bartender as I mixed with the reporters and photographers of the sports and news staffs of the four Toronto dailies: the *Star*, the *Mail and Empire*, the *Globe* and the *Evening Telegram*.

Among the photographers was Nat Turofsky, uncle of the future opera singer Riki Turofsky and, with his brother Lou, owner of Alexandra Studios, which specialized in sports photography. The *Star* had hired him to supply pictures of the swim.

Nat suggested a group photo. I thought he meant only the real newspeople, but he turned to me and said, "You, too, kid," inviting me to join the reporters and the uniformed policeman who had been assigned to the press tent.

I remember going home that night and proudly showing my mother my CNE press card, and excitedly telling her about the group picture, where I had stood in the company of all those hard-drinking, hard-driving reporters. For that moment, I was one of them. And I was proud. My parents, a Scottish mother and a Welsh father, who had built our house at 437 Clinton Street in 1904, didn't seem to understand my pride. They certainly weren't impressed by my boasts that I was part of the team that had covered the swim.

They had many more serious things on their minds. The Depression had put a stop to house building and there was no work for bricklayers, which was what my father was. The prospect of the Canada Permanent Mortgage Company not giving us another loan on our house was a perpetual nightmare for my mother and something my father said he didn't want to face. It would mean going on welfare, and to them, that was almost next to death.

As it was, the five dollars a week I paid my mother out of the six dollars I earned meant groceries. You couldn't carry five dollars' worth of food in those days. "Don't be late or do anything that might cause them to fire you," I remember my mother often saying after I got the job at the *Star*.

Eventually word came from the mortgage firm that they couldn't extend any more credit, and my parents had to swallow their pride and go on welfare. My twin brother, Gregor, was still going to Central Technical School, where I had attended partway into the second year before going to work, and my elder brother, Dave, was out every day, trying to find work. Although he was an experienced lineman and had worked for Ontario Hydro and Bell, any work he managed to get was only temporary.

Even though a large part of the neighborhood was on welfare (which in those days wasn't paid in cash, but in vouchers that got you bread, vegetables and few basics, but no meat), my mother wanted no one to know. So I had to take the vouchers to a distant shop, lest the neighbors see she was now on welfare, or the corner grocer, a man who minded everyone's business, tell people about it.

The fear of getting fired lasted most of my early years at the *Star*. Even when I became an experienced reporter, I dreaded the prospect of being scooped, and I think I can attribute my attitude to that ingrained plea from my mother not to lose my job. Of course, I also did not want to get fired because, even as a boy running copy for the reporters, I loved the work. I loved watching the newsmen, their hats tilted back on their heads, making the typewriter keys hop across the pages as they rushed off page after page for me and the other guys to take to the city desk.

My childhood had been spent in a home where discipline

reigned. My mother used to live in fear of a policeman coming to her front door because of something one of her sons had done. But even stealing apples from a neighbor's tree or grapes from backyard vines, which my chums and I did, was enough to bring police action. So my mother's fears were realized one day when I was around twelve or thirteen when Mrs. Sutton, the woman whose grapevines we were looting, walked to the nearby police station and reported that the grapes she brought to the cops were getting fewer and fewer because she was being robbed.

The next time we climbed her fence with a feast of grapes in mind, a husky Irish cop named Paddy Ward, whom I later came to know, was waiting. He wasn't quick enough to catch us, but as he chased us down the alley, he shouted, "I knay yer maither and I knay yer faither, and yer name is in the *book*."

He meant his notebook, and I found out that he knew my parents all right when I got home. He had already been there, and his call had shocked my mother so much that my father was angry at me for being the cause of it. He took it out on me, making me wish that Paddy had caught me and cuffed me around a couple of times and let that be the end of it.

Maybe it was a natural progression that I turned to newspaper work to make a living. At age ten, I was selling papers at Bloor and Bathurst streets to the workers coming home from the factories and shipyards at the foot of Bathurst. There was almost no news on radio in those days, and my customers depended on the papers, which sold for two cents apiece, for the very latest major league ball scores and race results. I also had a paper route with more than two hundred customers, in the days when carriers could sell both evening papers.

During the summer, I would buy both late editions from the same office and hawk them around the crowds watching the senior baseball games at Christie Pits, the popular name for Willowvale Park, at Christie and Bloor streets. The baseball scores and the results of races at Toronto and American tracks made it easy to sell about one hundred papers. Then, when the ball game was over and the papers were left on the grass, I picked them up, stored them in the garage and eventually sold them to a scrap dealer.

Church and activities connected with church took up any spare time. On Sunday mornings we went to nearby Saint Paul's Presbyterian Church because my mother was Scottish. In the afternoon there was Sunday school there, as well, followed by evening services at Dewi Sant (Saint David), the Welsh church a few blocks from our home. My mother declined to attend the services at Saint David, except when they were occasionally given in English. I was expected always to be on hand to pump the organ. There was no pay, but the stout, jovial Welshman who played the hymns always had a bag of candy. After the Sunday evening services, some of the men and a few of the women would gather for a sing-along in our living room. The Welsh sang at every opportunity they got.

Most of the congregation came from the coal mining area of Wales. My father had been down in the pits when he was thirteen, and he often said that the terrible conditions that had filled his lungs with coal dust had prepared him for the First World War, enabling him to survive a gas attack, one of the most flagrant of the atrocities of that grim conflict. His lungs must have been unusually strong, for he chain-smoked until he was well past eighty and only stopped because my mother was nagging him about spending so much money on cigarettes when they just had their old-age pensions to live on. He lived until he was ninety, the same as my mother, who was too frail to survive a broken hip.

Except for my twin brother, my closest companion was Art Stanley, who lived across the street. I always wanted to do what Art did, and when he said his uncle, a linotype operator and chairman of the union chapel at the *Star*, was going to get him into the shop as an apprentice printer, I said I'd like to go, too. That was October 1929.

The plan was to sign on as copy boys, because the *Star* needed dozens of them in those days to hike copy from the courts and for office boy duties. Art and I intended to do this until there were openings in the print shop. Both our turns came. Art eagerly accepted the opportunity. But by that time, I was having too much fun running out and being on a first-name basis with reporters like Gordon Sinclair, Athol Gow (the crime reporter, whom I was eventually to succeed) and a fine writer named Bill Shields. When the shop foreman told me I was next in line to go on the proof press, the first step in a printer's apprenticeship, I told him I had changed my mind.

2

My First Scoop

THAT FALL OF 1929 when I started out at the *Star*, the *Star* building was a gleaming new, twenty-three-story sky-scraper at 80 King Street West, said to be the third tallest building in the British Empire. It had cost $4 million, and Joseph E. Atkinson, the owner, quietly boasted to visiting newspaper tycoons that he'd had it all paid for before he moved in. To the staff, it was a well-kept secret that the Chief, as Atkinson was called, was not up to his neck in debt from his new building, which had opened just as the Great Depression hit.

Even at six dollars a week, I wasn't the lowest paid of the twenty-eight copy boys. That honor fell to John Hindmarsh, Atkinson's grandson and the son of Harry C. Hindmarsh, the *Star*'s legendary managing editor.

John, a muscular youth, who'd been a champion university boxer, got four dollars a week. His grandfather, who had complete charge of the payroll, apparently figured that that was all John needed, because his father got $225 a week, lived on an Oakville estate and drove a Pierce Arrow, which was just a little down the price range from Atkinson's sixteen-cylinder Cadillac.

I had seen many Hollywood movies about rough and tumble newsrooms and hard-hitting newsmen telling the cops how to solve the case or doing it themselves, but I had figured that such excitement was only possible in the United States. Imagine how pleased I was to discover that the *Star*'s newsroom was much like the ones in the movies and the reporters resembled their Hollywood counterparts, as well. Gordon Sinclair fit the image perfectly, wearing his fedora at a rakish angle and always leaving it on, indoors or out, as did most of the reporters. Sinclair was the highest paid, at $125 a week. The music critic, Augustus Bridle, was next to the top, at $100.

In those days before the other media came along, the blood and bones of newspapers was getting the news the quickest and beating your rivals to it. The *Star* put out six or seven editions a day, plus those that went to Hamilton and the suburbs; as incredible as it may seem now, it was possible for a story to be sent from a courtroom to the paper and be edited, printed and out on the street in hardly more than an hour. Thus, the newsroom was an incessant welter of activity, with the copy boys often being summoned to snatch a reporter's story as it emerged from his typewriter sheet by sheet.

The proceedings of important criminal trials and city council meetings were written in longhand and given to the copy boys, who streamed up and down Bay Street, to and from their papers. Sensational murder stories were written at great length, and sometimes it took two boys to handle the copy the reporter was churning out. When you picked up his pages, he always noted the time on them, and it was always checked by the head boy when you got to the paper. Some cases became so interesting as they evolved that I couldn't get down to the *Star* and back again quickly enough to suit me. On the way down, I would read the copy as I hustled along, and I began to understand how a court story was written.

Before being allowed to run copy on the street, however, I had to do time in the office. There wasn't enough bench space for all the boys, so we lined the walls, ready to sprint to the desk of a reporter when he shouted "boy." At least most of us sprinted. Hugh Garner, the future best-selling novelist, refused to run. He walked, to show his contempt for the shouted command.

The head boy was Red Burnett, who became a well-known

hockey writer, covering the Maple Leafs for many years. He was under instructions to keep the floor spotless, and we all dreaded his command to pick up the broom. Occasionally he got no answer when he told someone to sweep, and he only once gave the order to Hugh, who refused. "If you fire me, I'll bust your nose," he shouted, and Red knew he would, because he'd already had his nose bloodied in the parking lot by this tough kid from Cabbagetown.

Hugh didn't want to be a printer. He wanted to be a reporter, and almost made it the day he was walking a sheaf of copy down from Osgoode Hall and saw some excited men yelling at the people who were approaching city hall to get back. A Health Department employee had dropped a box of glass vials thought to contain highly contagious germs and a city hall reporter got the story after Hugh called in the tip. It was a page one scoop, and Hugh got a small bonus, though the story was later watered down to not much more than a lot of broken glass and a health officer assuring the public that there was no danger.

Hugh never got his chance to be a reporter. Shortly after the germ scoop, Red ordered him to do a job that he hated even more than sweeping the floor — guiding school kids through the building and reading from a booklet to tell them what they were seeing. Hugh refused. He was fired and he left, shouting obscenities on his way to the nearest pool room.

The incessant floor sweeping was in anticipation of Atkinson's inspection tours. Actually, he came around only a couple of times a month, until he had separate pull switches installed on the ceiling light fixtures. After that, he toured from office to office on bright days, turning off lights. As soon as he had disappeared, we turned them on again.

My mundane office duties were not much inspiration to a career in newspaper work, though the atmosphere was perpetually charged with the excitement of the next edition. Not only the reporters wore their hats as they worked. Most of the men who sat around the horseshoe-shaped desk, editing copy and writing heads, did so, as well. Those who didn't wore green eyeshades and elbow garters. Copy boys wore knickerbockers, long black stockings that went above the knees, tight-fitting, hip-length jackets and peaked caps.

There were female writers on the *Star*, but none in the city room because Atkinson didn't want them to hear the male reporters' rough language. So even Alexandrine Gibb, who covered women's police court and later wrote a sports column, was segregated with the women who wrote the wedding stories and social notes. This was the big difference I noticed between life at the *Star* and life in Hollywood movies, where the sob sister and the ace reporter often teamed up to win the day.

By mid-morning, with the eleven o'clock deadline for the noon edition approaching, the turmoil in the city room became feverish. Every telephone was in use. Since no females were allowed, the cord switchboard was operated by a copy boy, who shouted out the names of the reporters, making sure he used the word "Mister." As often as not, the reporters shouted back that the boy had cut them off, which was easily accomplished, as I found out when it was my turn on the board.

The deadlines for the various editions fell about two hours apart, so the excitement continued for most of the day — until five p.m. in winter and, in summer, till six o'clock, so the major league baseball scores would be complete on the scoreboard that ran across the front page. Yet, as stimulating as the newsroom was, I found the real excitement and glamour in the courtrooms, especially when a murder trial was underway. I never tired of listening to and reading the reporter's accounts of the adversarial interplay between the Crown and defense lawyers, each fighting his hardest to make his point to the jury.

Judges, on the other hand, frightened me. This was a quite palpable fear that began the day I showed up in court after my father had resoled my shoes since we didn't have money for new ones. As I tiptoed down the aisle to the table where the reporter was writing his story, each step was punctuated by a squeak that sounded like a rasp file. The judge, Mr. Justice Nicol Jeffrey of the Ontario Supreme Court, stopped a lawyer in mid-sentence and turned his and the whole courtroom's attention on me, then yelled that I was to get out and not come back with those abominable shoes. I grabbed the copy and slunk out to the distinct sounds of giggling.

Back at the *Star*, I told Red that the judge had told me not to come back with the noisy shoes. "Take them off before you go in," he said.

At the courtroom, the sheriff's officer at the door, who was a retired Toronto policeman, gave me a wink as I slipped my shoes off and walked in. I feared that the judge might see me in my stocking feet with a toe protruding from a hole. But he was turned toward the witness stand and gave no indication that he saw me. The next day, I returned wearing socks without holes, but the same shoes, from which the squeak had been removed by a little stretching. Who had two pairs of shoes in the Depression?

The Depression was *the* major fact of life, and I soon had to face the additional fact that copy boys who had not made their mark and earned a trial as a reporter were laid off when they reached the age of nineteen.

My break came not long after the 1930 CNE swim, when I was assigned to run copy from what was then known as the County Police Court, near King and Church, the only trial court at that time that was not in city hall. The reporter was a law student who worked for the *Star* in the morning and attended classes in the afternoon. One morning he had an exam and didn't show up. The *Tely* reporter who usually covered the court, apparently aware that the *Star* guy wasn't going to be there, didn't show, either. No one had told me not to show up, so I sat alone at the press table, wondering how I would tell Red that I had no copy.

The session began, and there was a clatter of footsteps as a prisoner climbed the stairs to the dock from the cells below. I recognized him as a man who had been on trial a couple of weeks earlier for molesting little girls. Magistrate William Keith, a kindly, soft-spoken man, who was one of the many magistrates in those days who had not graduated in law, but had come from the civilian ranks, began to speak. I began writing.

Keith said that the man had been warned many times that his jail term would be increased if he didn't cease his attacks on children. He had not stopped. He was too dangerous ever to be allowed free again. Therefore, the only way to ensure the community's safety was to send him to Kingston Penitentiary for the rest of his natural life.

There were gasps in the courtroom.

My instincts told me to get to the telephone fast, and I was soon talking to the city editor, telling him that I'd written down what the magistrate had said. For good measure, I had also spoken to the detective on the case and picked up more details from C. Frank Moore, the Crown attorney.

My story was the banner headline in the first edition that morning. A scoop in the days when scoop was king!

When I got back to the office, the news editor, John Drylie, an excitable man who was always on the jump and constantly fighting with the composing room foreman over last-minute stories getting in the paper, rushed over as I came through the door. As I walked to the copy boys' bench, he patted my back and said, "Good work, laddie."

My headline remained for another two editions, and I couldn't have felt better if I had scored a world beat. Later Drylie called me aside and said I was getting a two-dollar-a-week raise. Raises were few and far between in those days, and I was elated.

3

My Innocence Wanes

THE SCOOP AND THE TWO-DOLLAR RAISE earned me the right to come in an hour early to try my hand at scalps — rewriting stories from the morning papers. When I saw my rewrites in the *Star* exactly as I had written them, or with minor corrections, I had no regrets about having turned down the printing apprenticeship.

Eventually I was assigned to work with Roly Young, the features editor. He appointed me horoscope editor, which was simply a typing job. Readers sent in their birth dates and I matched them with passages in a syndicated book the *Star* subscribed to. The feature filled two or three columns every day. It was very popular, and Roly once showed me a letter from a service club, inviting the horoscope editor to give a talk at one of their luncheons. How could they have known that the horoscope editor was a boy of seventeen, still in knickerbockers?

Another of my duties was putting out the children's page, which was bought from a syndicate, as well. It had to be edited and the headings written according to our style, and when it didn't fill a *Star* page, I had to turn out some copy. I also ran the Young Rangers Club. Kids would send in ten cents and they'd get a little bronze pin to wear, and periodically we'd have games in High Park and other gatherings for them. It was all necessary experience, but, needless to say, I was very happy when I was sent back to the courts.

The training ground for cub reporters in those days were the magistrates' courts at city hall, where I served a period covering liquor and traffic trials presided over by a strong temperance man who wrote hymns as he listened to the cases. Then, in 1932, I was assigned to the women's police court, where all sex offenses were heard. Until then it had been covered by Alexandrine Gibb, who had chaperoned and written about the highly successful Canadian women's team at the 1928 Olympics.

The women's court was presided over by Magistrate Margaret Patterson, who had no legal training. She had distinguished herself in social work. Defense lawyers continually complained that her rulings were at variance with the evidence and that she wrongly applied the law, but she seldom listened to their arguments and curtly cut them off with a rap of the gavel and a finding of guilty.

Keepers of bawdy houses and the women who worked in them all got jail terms. Sexual attacks and incest invariably brought eight years in the penitentiary. One day she became annoyed because I didn't lower my voice while speaking to another reporter at the press table. "Get out!" she shouted. I retreated toward the door, where the burly policeman who stood there gave me an extra shove to help me on my way. I returned the next day, too frightened even to look at the stern magistrate. She survived many controversies and much criticism from appeal court judges, but people said she was best for the job.

Being at women's court meant that I had a place in the paper every day, where the court news was printed under a special heading. Often I ended up with a whole column, even though the explicit evidence in the incest, rape, sexual assault and bestiality cases, along with the raids on the whorehouses, had to be couched in gentle terms. For instance, buggery was simply "a serious offense." And although rape was a Criminal Code charge and still a capital offense, the *Star* always called it "a serious charge involving a woman." On the other hand, rape and incest victims' names *were* printed. It never occurred to anyone that a woman might not want to tell her story in front of a crowded courtroom.

I also saw many women and a few doctors face charges connected with abortion. One doctor, who had caused the death of a socialite, got seven years in Kingston. I reported that he had "performed an illegal operation."

It was a whole new world to me.

On one of my first days there, I had to ask Major Davies, the senior reporter for the *Evening Telegram*, who was sitting at the press table, what incest was. I had never heard the term. He looked at me rather askance, then sneered, "I'm not a nursemaid for *Star* reporters." I realized that he might have been put off by my youth or simply hated the *Star*, but his words stung me to the quick.

Anyway, I found out what incest was soon enough, for the evidence that the daughter gave against her father was, to say the least, graphic. In most incest cases, though, the court simply heard a guilty plea after the defendant's statement to the police had been read out by the Crown attorney.

Regardless of their length, incest trials were pitiful things to watch. I am sure the accused never had any idea of the severe sentences they were about to get. Most of the time they were stunned, and the mother would be screaming, and the girl would be pleading, "Don't send him to jail. Don't send him to jail."

"Eight years," Magistrate Patterson would say. "Take him away. Next case."

Justice was especially swift in those days for the poor, and even with time off for good behavior, an eight-year sentence meant spending the best part of six years in Kingston. Many of the people I saw had no legal counsel. There was no Legal Aid. If you didn't have a lawyer, that was too bad, Jake, though in some cases you might be assigned what was then known as a "pauper's counsel," usually a lawyer who was on the skids.

There was never any suggestion that sex offenders were sick. They were just no good, and the sentences were severe. In county police court, I once covered a trial where one of four boys who had been convicted of raping a girl in York

Township had iron braces on his legs from polio. That saved him from getting the twenty lashes that were given his companions, but not from the fifteen-year term that each of the four got.

If you got twenty years in those days, it meant something like sixteen years, four months and so many days, and that was the absolute minimum. In magistrates' courts, I often heard judges tell violent criminals, "That'll be five years in Kingston Penitentiary and ten lashes. If you don't want the lashes, it's another five years." The courts didn't have any jurisdiction over this, but if lashes were added to a prisoner's sentence, a portion of them were administered when he entered the prison. Partway through the term, he got another portion, then about two months before his release, he got the rest, just so he wouldn't forget why he'd been in there.

The weird thing was that throughout this long initiation in the rigors and horrors of the criminal justice system, I was still doing the horoscopes and the children's page. In those days, newspapers were sweatshops. After working all day, you went out and covered meetings at night. There was no overtime, of course, but if your meeting started before eight o'clock, you could put in a claim for fifty cents for your supper, and you got streetcar tickets. I covered many CCF meetings. The party had only recently been formed, and the *Star* (which was then known in business circles as "the Red *Star* of 80 King West" because of the large space devoted to stories lauding Soviet socialism) was giving it a lot of coverage.

About 1933, I bought a Ford roadster with the proceeds from a tip on a fixed horse race at the old track near College and Dufferin streets. Gas cost twenty-five cents a gallon, so I sold my streetcar tickets in the composing room and drove to the meetings, often with my girlfriend, Marjorie Stanley, who is now my wife. The meetings were often held in parks, rather than halls. Marjorie, who knew shorthand, would take notes. Then we would go back to the *Star*, and she would dictate the story for me to type.

Most days, you were never free until around half past ten, maybe eleven o'clock, which was why I didn't mind being assigned to the night police reporter's job. You had to work all night, but you didn't have to attend meetings in the evening. I started in 1933, shortly after I saw my first murder victim.

It was early morning, before the courts opened. Athol Gow had got the tip, and I was sent over to a print shop on Duke Street. I arrived ahead of the other reporters and got right into the office, where a man was lying dead of a gunshot wound to the head, his blood all over the floor. The cops had the clutch on a guy just down the hall.

The other employees told me that the two men had worked side by side, and a few months before this, the man down the hall had stopped speaking to the other guy. He began talking to himself, often muttering the other guy's name. The dead man, the employees said, had done absolutely nothing to provoke the fellow. But he had developed a feeling that the victim hated him and had a gun in his pocket and was waiting for an opportunity to kill him, so he went out and got a gun of his own and shot him.

I couldn't *believe* that that could happen. I couldn't accept the fact that one man could kill another without any provocation whatever. I didn't understand that the man must have gone crazy. I was still very naive. And confused. But that was only the first part of my introduction to police reporting that day, for I then had to go to the victim's house and get a photograph.

I got there before the police, as reporters sometimes did in those days. The standard procedure in such events, I later learned, was to make an excuse and back off. There was always a chance that if you broke the news yourself, the person you were talking to would collapse. Which was what had happened once after a fatal bus crash in Barrie. A reporter tracked down a victim's wife and called up to her, "Are you the widow Brown?" She fell down a flight of stairs, breaking a limb, which cost the *Star* $1,500.

In the case of the Duke Street printer's widow, I just blundered awkwardly ahead. I said I'd just been downtown to where he worked. I said he might have had some kind of collapse. He might even have been shot. I wasn't sure. I didn't let on that I'd actually seen him lying on the floor. "He's dead, anyway," I said. "Is there a picture of him?" Fortunately another lady lived in the house, a relative of some kind, I think. She comforted the devastated woman, and they got me the picture.

Getting crime and accident victims' photographs was always a distasteful thing, and I never got used to it.

4

The Night Police Beat

POLICE HEADQUARTERS was then at 149 College Street. Previously the building had been the first Central Technical School, and my father had gone there to brush up on his bricklaying skills when he came back from the First World War.

The press had a little room with a couple of desks in it on the third floor, quite close to the detective department and right next to the elevator. If the detectives were rushing out on something, you could corner them and say, "Where ya going?" and they'd often answer, "To some murder."

They had to bring their prisoners up in the elevator, and we could always have a cameraman there if anyone newsworthy was being brought in. On more than one summer night, with the window open, we heard gunshots on nearby Queen's Park Crescent. Charlie Oliver, the *Globe*'s police reporter, would look up and say, "Trigger Payne." And sure enough, about twenty minutes later, the elevator would open and Constable Adolphus Payne of the auto squad would emerge with yet another car thief he had nailed by shooting out the guy's tires. There were no restrictions on the police use of firearms then. Some two decades later, I would several times describe Payne in the stories I wrote about him as Canada's greatest detective.

But we didn't just sit around all night, waiting for cops like Payne to bring the news to us. A huge part of my job was dashing here and there in a *Star* car, chasing ambulances, police cars and fire trucks. Toronto was a much smaller place then, and even store awning fires were reported.

Stickups were, if anything, more prevalent then than they are today. United Cigar Stores and the Laura Secord and Jenny Lind candy shops used to stay open late and were regularly held up, along with grocery stores and gas stations. Later in the decade, women's hosiery shops began staying open in the evening, as well, and they got robbed, too.

It was a nail-biting existence, waiting for the morning newspapers to see what you had missed. If you *had* missed something, you paid for it by being paraded before the city editor and asked a lot of questions you couldn't answer. Personal contact was the name of the game, and it took a long period of telephoning and visiting the different police stations, hospital emergency wards, fire department dispatchers, the city morgue and other news sources, before results began to show in my work.

The best personal contacts, of course, were the police. But first they had to learn to trust you, particularly in instances where they told you about a developing case and you promised not to write it up until an arrest had been made. As Athol Gow warned me when I started, "If you double-cross any of them, the word will go around in no time at all and you'll be useless."

But it was Charlie Oliver who really taught me about being a police reporter and how to get along with the cops. "Never buck the police," he told me. "Don't argue with them. They don't have any legal obligation to give you news. If you can't get information from one guy, don't lose your temper. You can always get it somewhere else — from another police source or out on the street."

Similarly cops used to say to me, "Lookit, Jocko, watch Charlie Oliver, the way he does things. Do it his way and you'll be as popular as he is."

As a result of that mutual trust and respect, the police let Charlie in on all kinds of things that they kept from the rest of us. For instance, around that time a bearded lawyer named W. Perkins Bull somehow hooked up with a Mrs. Horlick of the wealthy Chicago malted milk family. He was something of a Svengali, and she died in his Rosedale home in a room that had bars on the windows. When an inquest was ordered, the *Globe* was the only paper to get a picture of Bull receiving his subpoena because the detective who was working on the investigation told Charlie exactly what time to have a cameraman ready.

The detective went to Bull's house about eleven p.m. and rapped on the door. Charlie and John Boyd, the photographer, were hiding behind a pillar. Bull came downstairs and opened the door, wearing a long, flowing nightshirt and one of those long nightcaps men used to wear. Boyd stepped away from the pillar. His flash went *boom!* as they used to do in those days, and on the front page of the *Globe*'s next edition, under a heading that said SUMMONS AT MIDNIGHT, was a dandy picture of W. Perkins Bull receiving a subpoena in his nightcap. The inquest found that Mrs. Horlick's death was from natural causes, though there was a hint that she had been neglected.

That was in the days when the police never even let us look at the blotter, their record of arrests and charges. Today blotter information is given out in regular press releases. At that time, a policeman might read an arrested person's name off the official blotter for you, but that was it. Sometimes, though, if you craned your neck a bit, you got a look at a blotter page and saw the words "not to be given to the press" typed in red. That meant there was somebody's name there that they didn't want out, but with a little digging, you usually found out who it was.

In other words, although the trust and cooperation of the police were an indispensable part of the job, you were not there to write only stories that they approved of. You were there on behalf of your paper, and over the years I wrote many stories that the police would have rather not seen in print. In fact, around the time I started on the night police beat, the day reporters were infuriating a lot of cops by writing up the exploits of the Hundred Percent Gang, a band of crooked constables and a sergeant, who had been methodically looting downtown stores, either breaking into them or using stolen keys.

The gang's name came from their pledge that if any of them were ever caught, the others would look after his family. One of the thieves was eventually caught and went to Kingston Penitentiary thinking that his wife and kids would be taken care of. But she soon wrote and told him that his friends had completely ignored her pleas for money to buy food for the children and pay the rent. The former policeman wrote to the police chief, and the lid was off. A royal commission revealed details of the gang's activities and the often amusing stories of how it had been apprehended. For instance, a lawyer for one of the town's finest shoe merchants had figured out that policemen might be responsible for the store's missing stock because most of the stolen shoes were of very large sizes.

Although they had no sympathy for the thieves, the police did not appreciate the constant play the story was getting in the press, and reporters on all four papers, but especially the *Star*, got rough treatment from them. My turn came while I was looking into a tragedy on Queen Street West that I had discovered during a check of the hospital emergency wards.

That afternoon, a man had been stationed to keep people from going into a second-story flat that had just been fumigated. He had a bottle of wine with him and soon passed out in the hot sun, falling off his leaned-back chair. Two kiddies who lived around the corner and had been playing on Queen Street stepped over him and climbed the stairs to their deaths.

I found their mother in a nearby house with her best friend, who agreed to get me pictures of the children. I was standing well back from the room where the mother was being comforted, when a large police sergeant, who was called Cherry Nose by his colleagues, came into the house. He saw me taking notes and demanded to know my newspaper affiliation. I said the *Star* and reached for my police pass, which had my photo and the signature of the chief constable on it. Cherry Nose grabbed me by the scruff of the neck, marched me out to the veranda and tossed me bodily onto the pavement.

I waited in the car and got the pictures after he had gone. Even so, I returned to headquarters feeling horribly deflated. Charlie was there. "Don't let it worry you, kid," he said. "It's a long lane that doesn't have any ash cans."

My first big night police story came not long after that, when a sergeant on the headquarters desk told me that two Ontario Provincial Police officers had asked permission to book two men for planning to kidnap J. S. McLean, the president of Canada Packers and a man known all across Canada. I ran over to the OPP office at Queen's Park, which was just a few blocks away. The reporters from the morning papers were already there, getting the story. But they had to rush off to meet their early deadlines. That left me alone to ask a few more questions, which the officers were reluctant to answer. However, as I was leaving, one young constable said, "Get out to the Palace Cabins on the Lakeshore."

The light was still on in the motel owner's living quarters when I arrived with a *Star* cameraman. The owner took us to a cabin that had been rented by two men a week before. The floor had been partially torn out and there was a hole in the ground containing a cot and a box that held a supply of food. This was where McLean was to have been held while his ransom was negotiated.

I wrote the story at the *Star*, banging it out and shouting for a boy the way the seasoned reporters had done when I was running their copy to the city desk. As I worked, I heard Vernon Knowles, the new managing editor, ask the assistant city editor, "Who is that reporter?" He was, I realized, impressed by the exclusive part about the hole in the cabin, which wasn't in either of the morning papers, and the plot to kidnap McLean was the big headline story of the day.

As I was putting on my coat to go home a couple of hours after the normal quitting time, Knowles, a soft-spoken man whom Atkinson had hired away from the *Mail and Empire* because he thought Hindmarsh was working too hard, came over to me and said, "Good work, son." When the next pay envelope came through, I felt I was in clover. My salary had been raised to twelve dollars a week!

The young constable who gave me the tip about the cabins was named Jimmy Bartlett. About twenty-five years later, he would be a deputy OPP commissioner, and I would write a series of articles about gambling clubs, provoking a royal commission into organized crime that would reveal that he had been bribed by gamblers.

5

Labatt Blues

SCOOPS UNDOUBTEDLY SOLD PAPERS, but I often suspected that their main purpose was to enable the managing editor of the paper with the latest scoop to sit in his office chortling over the discomfort of his opposite numbers at the other papers.

Nevertheless, in my early days at the *Star* we lived in fear of being scooped. If a reporter at another paper got lucky and came up with a big scoop, or got one through ingenuity and guile, you could be forgiven. But Hindmarsh was a great believer in reporters sticking to their posts. If they were away from their posts or were otherwise careless and got scooped, they were fired. This cloud was always with us, and together with a natural combativeness it often drove us to almost comic-opera frenzies of effort to beat the *Evening Telegram*. Our response to the 1934 kidnapping of the brewing magnate John Sackville Labatt is a good case in point. But first I must tell you about how, around that time, I scooped myself and came close to being fired.

My friend Sid Hibbs was the *Tely*'s night police reporter. He had a girlfriend downtown and often spent the night with her after asking me to cover for him.

One night there was a fire in an old east end church that had been taken over by a scrap metal dealer. Not much of a story, it seemed. But when I got there, the district fire chief and a neighbor told me that this was really a historic spot, one of the first churches in old Muddy York. I went down to the *Star* library and dug up some information about the church, which I incorporated in a nice story about the fire at this historical landmark. The night editor was not impressed. He had no taste for history. Also, there was no human element — nobody burned, nobody rescued, no dogs or cats or any of the other story ingredients that the *Star* thrived on. So he chopped the piece down to a very small, routine fire item.

I found that out only later, because I was busy writing a similar story for Sid. Of course, he didn't come back to headquarters at all that morning, and I put the story in the *Tely*'s mailbox for him, thinking that was the end of it.

That afternoon, the *Telegram* gave Sid's church fire story a prominent place on page three, and I received a clipping of it, attached to a note from John R. Heron, the city editor. It said, "This is the kind of story we expect our night police reporter to turn out. Not *this* one." Also attached was the little patch of an item that had run in the back pages of the *Star*.

Naturally there was no way I could say, "*I* wrote the *Tely* story." I just had to take my lumps. But I did show him a duplicate of my original piece. "I had everything that was in the *Tely*," I said.

As he read the dupe, he said, "Gee, some of the stuff in the *Telegram* is very much like what you have."

"Oh, is it?" I said, as innocently as I could.

The Labatt saga began on a hot August day with an exclusive tip from Arthur Carty, a freelance reporter and photographer in London. He said John Labatt had been kidnapped near London and his car abandoned on a side road. A ransom note, demanding $150,000 and signed by someone who called himself Three-fingered Abe, had been left on the front seat.

When the tip came in, John Drylie, the news editor, leaped out of his chair and yelled, "No one uses the phone. Only incoming calls." He knew there were men on the desk who made extra money stringing for the U.S. wire services, and he was protecting the *Star*'s beat.

Larger-than-usual headlines were flashed across the front page of the next edition. It was a clean scoop, the biggest the

Star had scored since 1928, when it had beat the world with pictures of the *Bremen*, the transatlantic aircraft that had crashed on a small island off Labrador.

Our scoop threw the *Telegram* newsroom into a panic. The almost incoherent city editor, Herb Berkley, called Fred Egan, the *Tely*'s day reporter at police headquarters, demanding something on the kidnapping. As far as Egan was concerned, it was a London story, but he dutifully went looking for the chief of detectives, John Chisholm.

He learned that Chisholm was in conference with the chief of police, Dennis C. Draper, and a well-dressed man who had been in a rush to see the chief. Egan glanced out the window to the parking lot and noticed a Cadillac parked in a reserved spot. Yes, Draper's secretary said, that was the hurried man's car. A quick check with the motor vehicle registration office revealed the owner's name: Hugh Labatt, brother of the kidnapped brewer.

LABATT KIDNAPPERS OPEN NEGOTIATIONS IN TORONTO was the way the *Tely* headlined Egan's story in the largest type they had. No one had actually told Egan that negotiations had opened, but it was a good assumption, given the fact that the police chief and the chief of detectives had been closeted with the kidnapped man's brother for well over an hour.

Chief Draper refused to say anything, wouldn't even admit he had met Labatt. He did, though, call a press conference for seven p.m. in his office. Before him was a copy of the pink *Tely* with its blaring headline. Pointing to it, he went into a rage, accusing the newspaper of subverting the course of justice, being irresponsible and a few other things, until Egan asked, "Sir, is the story *right*?"

"Yes. That's what's *wrong* with it!" Draper shouted, and pounded the desk, causing his ink pot to jump and spill onto his trousers. There was a burst of laughter and we filed out.

The *Tely*'s scoop had, of course, thrown the *Star* into a panic. But we soon learned that Hugh Labatt was registered at the Royal York Hotel. One of our reporters, Major Claud Pascoe, OBE, who was a great guy for fixing things, got the room right next to Labatt's by bribing somebody at the hotel and having the occupants moved elsewhere. We were smug.

What we didn't know was that Percy Cole of the *Telegram* had also bribed somebody and got the room on the other side.

Hugh Labatt spoke in a very loud voice, and neither group of reporters had any trouble hearing him take a call, then phone the police and say he had been instructed to throw the money over the Humber bridge. He didn't say *which* Humber bridge, and that was the night we found out how many bridges there were over the Humber River. There were more bridges than there were reporters. But as many bridges as possible were staked out in the hope that someone would be on hand for the ransom payment.

The *Star's* Doug Blanchard was sent to cover the Lambton Bridge on Dundas Street West. He waited near a service station. As he described the scene in his colorfully written front page story the next day, a car came rushing up, and two obviously drunk men jumped out and dashed into the service station. They spoke to the attendant for a few minutes, called someone on the phone, then staggered back to their car and raced away. Blanchard immediately cornered the attendant, who said the men had not identified themselves; they were unshaven and quite inebriated; *and* they could very well have been the kidnappers, because when they were on the phone, one of them had said something like "Labatt ain't here."

Another scoop for the *Star*! At the *Telegram*, Herb Berkley had a fit and bawled out Fred Egan and another reporter. "You guys were assigned to that bridge. How come *you* didn't see this?"

Egan and the other man had nothing to say.

"I mean," Egan later told me, "how could we tell him those two drunks Blanchard wrote about were *us*?"

The call to Hugh Labatt turned out to be a hoax. No money was thrown over any bridge, and the police, who were furious with both us and the guy who had called, later arrested a local rounder named Tutty and charged him with public mischief. He had simply read about Hugh Labatt in the paper, called the big hotels until he got the right one and put in his request.

No ransom was ever paid for John Labatt. As we later learned, he had been taken blindfolded to a Muskoka cottage, where he was handcuffed to a bed while efforts were made to collect the ransom. These failed and he was driven to North Toronto. He took a taxi to the Royal York and walked through the lobby without any of the reporters who were staking the place out seeing him.

Many cynics believed that the Labatt kidnapping wasn't the real thing. Afterward, "Gimme me a pint of the Missing Man" was an often-heard request in the beverage rooms. It fueled a rumor, proven in the end to be ridiculous, that Labatt had faked the kidnapping to advertise his beer.

The police did not know anyone named Three-fingered Abe. However, when Labatt was shown the OPP rogues' gallery of mug shots, he picked out David Meisner of London and later identified him in a lineup as one of his kidnappers. Meisner went on trial before the Ontario Supreme Court in February 1935, and mainly on the dramatic courtroom identification by Labatt, the jury found him guilty. He was sentenced to fifteen years.

Six months later, the OPP got word that the whole thing had been a mistake. The Detroit police had learned through underworld sources that the kidnapping had been the work of three Windsor men: James Bannon and Russell Knowles, two criminals who worked both sides of the border, and Michael McCardell, who was missing two fingers on one hand and known as Three-fingered Abe.

The Labatt story remained news for well over two years and didn't die out until after Meisner's suit for false imprisonment was settled. He sought $50,000 in damages, but an out-of-court agreement gave him $15,000.

The J. S. McLean and Labatt kidnap stories are early memories of excitement on the crime beat. You eagerly waited for news like that to break.

6

Draper

IT IS RATHER FITTING that General Dennis C. Draper, Toronto's chief of police from 1928 to 1946, should have made his first appearance in these memoirs in a scene where an ink pot jumps off a desk and spills onto his trousers. For just as John Chisholm, Draper's chief of detectives and eventual successor, was the best (and most tragic) police chief Toronto ever had, Draper was clearly the most incompetent and clownish.

To Draper, the fight against crime was as simple as finding the enemy on the battlefield. For example, a lot of crime during his early years as chief was blamed on a gang of brothers named Campbell. One day, Draper called the detective squad in and lined them all up for an inspection of their revolvers. Some of their bullets were corroded green from nonuse, so he sent them away to shine up the shells. "That's better," he said when they had reassembled. He then revealed the real purpose of the meeting. "You know as well as I do that the Campbells are doing all these crimes. I want them *shot!*" He shouted the last word.

The detectives couldn't believe it. They knew they had no right to shoot anybody unless they were in danger. And anyway, the chief had not put his finger on the main problem. As one of the detectives later remarked, "He wants them shot, and we can't even find them."

I rarely had anything to do with Draper, except for the occasional, odd encounter. For instance, on a hot August Sunday in 1936, Lou Appleby, owner of the Roxy burlesque theater on Queen Street, near Bay, was found murdered. It being Sunday, there was no burlesque, and the theater had been rented by a Chinese company, which was staging an opera with lots of Oriental music and colorful dragon costumes. The murdered man was in the office upstairs, shot to death, his safe door open.

Toronto had only about seven murders a year in those days, and Draper's orders were that he be summoned to each one. The detectives used to say, "What's the use waiting for Draper? He doesn't know anything about police work, anyhow." But that was the rule.

I was there with a photographer, waiting to get a photo of the body being removed. Detective Sergeant Fred Storm was in charge of the case.

The coroner, Dr. Julian Loudon, was also there, and he wanted the body right away. "I've released it," he insisted. "We're waiting to do the autopsy."

"Doesn't matter," Storm replied. "The old man's gotta be here."

But no one seemed to know where the old man was. He finally arrived well after dark, carrying a big electric lantern. I told the photographer to get a picture of him going into the theater. However, when Draper saw the cameraman, he ran at him, swinging his lantern and barking, "Outa the way, outa the way!" We got a good picture of that, and it ran in the paper.

Draper was not a policeman.

He had been hired after the police commission decided that the force needed a strict military disciplinarian in the chief's office. They approached the Department of Defense in Ottawa and were directed to Dennis C. Draper, a retired brigadier general and defeated Conservative candidate who was working for a Quebec paper company. He was given the job over the heads of a popular deputy chief and a chief inspector. One of his first public utterances was that criminals and gamblers could expect to be jailed and given the lash.

When Draper arrived in Toronto, he was met at Union Station and brought to city hall, where the police and suitably frocked civic dignitaries awaited him. There was a buzz when he got out of the car and everyone saw how short he was in comparison with the tall strapping officers who greeted him. A *Tely* reporter turned to Athol Gow and exclaimed, "Gow, he's a *midget*!"

At that time, the police force was dominated by Anglo-Saxon Protestants, most of them from Scotland and Northern Ireland. They made good police officers in the days when rawboned treatment of the criminal was judged the best way to law and order. To get ahead on the force, you had to be either a Mason or a member of the Orange Order, preferably both. In that respect, the police department wasn't any different from other civic departments. You needed some kind of political connection even to be considered for a civil service job. Wages of policemen and firemen were very good, and there was a pension, too, something rare in industry in those days.

Gow told me that, initially, the city's newsmen feared they would not get much cooperation from the new chief because he wouldn't understand their work. Draper fooled them. He sought their confidence and, for a while, got along well with them. He asked them many questions about the force and the cliques that dominated it. When a major crime occurred, he would summon the reporters from the press room and go to the scene with them, something the previous chief hadn't done.

And, initially, Draper did a lot of good for the force as far as breaking up the fraternal connection that was necessary for promotion. But he never forgot an officer he didn't like. I remember one man who was an acting detective for sixteen years without ever being promoted to the full rank because of some little thing that had irritated Draper.

His ignorance of police work and the fact that he had been parachuted in over their heads caused the police brass to dislike him from the start. The rank and file grew to hate him for the fierce discipline he imposed. There was a police association, or union, but it was weak, and Draper dominated it to such an extent that the men rebelled and held a strike vote.

In those days, police disciplinary hearings were held in secret, but word of Draper's harsh penalties soon leaked out. Gow got lots of tips. For example, one winter Draper tried an officer who, while walking his beat on a terrible, subzero night, slipped into the back of a restaurant for a coffee. He was fined an exorbitant ten days' pay. Somebody told Gow, and the *Star* ran a big story about this poor, freezing policeman.

The enmity of some senior members of the force was such that they looked for opportunities to tip off the newspapers when Draper blundered, as he did when he ordered the withdrawal of a drunk driving charge laid against the son of a federal Tory cabinet minister. A police chief who did that today would be finished. Understandably, Draper came to loathe the press.

But, even though there were constant calls for his resignation and he was opposed by all the newspapers except the *Globe*, Draper held his job for an amazingly long time. The reason for this soon became clear. Toronto's business leaders, the Eatons and the other big wheels who really ran the city, thought he would save them from Communism.

The Depression was at its height. Families were starving, and agitators had little trouble increasing the discontent. These were the days of relief riots, when municipal councillors, especially in the townships of York and East York, were besieged by mobs demanding increased welfare. Fiery speeches were made every Sunday in Queen's Park, and Draper, nudged by his business friends, decided he would break up the Reds with his mounted squad. These officers came to be called Draper's Dragoons, and he himself rode at the head of them.

I was on duty at the *Star* one Sunday afternoon when a group of men came into the office with blood pouring from head cuts they had received from the Dragoons, who had charged through Queen's Park. They had beaten everyone there on the assumption that anyone in the park had to be a Communist. The victims also went to the *Mail and Empire* along the street and the *Tely* around the corner. They complained that they had been innocent bystanders, as no doubt many of them were, sitting on the park benches and not particularly drawn there by the radicals' exhortation to rise up against the capitalists of the world.

All three papers ran the victims' pictures and stories of police brutality. Draper was incensed. To him, the newspapers were just as bad as the agitators. The *Star* editorials that said public parks were there for people to enjoy without being beaten on their heads with police batons and accused of being Communists particularly infuriated him.

He and Gow had long since stopped speaking. But one day, enraged by something in the *Star*, Draper sent for Gow and angrily shouted that he should tell Joseph E. Atkinson, the paper's owner, that he was "coining money from Bolshevism." Gow grabbed the telephone at Draper's elbow, called Atkinson's office and, handing the phone to Draper, said, "Here, tell him yourself." Draper didn't. Atkinson laughed heartily when Gow told him Draper's comment.

Draper's business and political connections even enabled him to survive the notorious Dorland case, which unfolded shortly before I was assigned to police headquarters. It started with an informer named Toohey telling the police that a robber named Albert Dorland had asked him to get some guns so they could hold up a bank on Church Street, just north of Maple Leaf Gardens. The chief of detectives, with Draper's permission, arranged for Toohey to be given some pistols.

A squad of detectives was assigned to watch the bank on the appointed day, but not all of them had been told about the arrangement with Toohey. Only members of Draper's clique were in on the "frame-up," as the escapade was called in the report of the subsequent royal commission.

Dorland and Toohey entered the bank. But at the last moment, Dorland became suspicious, and he and Toohey rushed out of the bank and raced away in their car without having initiated the holdup. The police gave chase. As they sped along Wellesley Street, the detectives, thinking there *had* been a holdup, opened fire. Dorland and Toohey were captured, and the next day Dorland pleaded guilty to robbery and was given fifteen years. Toohey was later given a short reformatory term, of which he served only a very small part. It had been all arranged for him to sort of go in the front door and out the back.

After Dorland's conviction, an editorial in Draper's friend, the *Globe*, praised the police under the heading ANOTHER OFF TO KINGSTON PEN. But word of the frame-up, perhaps from Dorland himself, got to the attorney general, William H. Price. Price didn't like Draper for some reason. Perhaps he was appalled by the fact that bank employees and bystanders could have been slaughtered by criminals wielding guns that had been given to them by the police. At any rate, he ordered the royal commission.

The report by Mr. Justice Kingstone blistered the force and accused some of the brass of lying in the witness box. Draper, it was shown, had known about the plot from the start, but the chief of detectives, a man named Murray, became the fall guy. He resigned on pension, and one of the detectives, Archie McCathie, was charged with shooting with intent to kill or wound Dorland. He was acquitted in a jury trial. Later McCathie became a deputy chief.

Dorland was freed from jail, but public sympathy was wasted. Not long afterward, he was nailed for a $25,000 bank robbery in the west Toronto stockyards area. After the term he served for that was up, the RCMP caught him trafficking in heroin.

The nearest Draper came to losing his job occurred in the mid-thirties when William Stewart, a staunch Orange Order man, was mayor. At that time, the mayor of Toronto chaired a three-member police commission, on which also sat two county court judges. Draper was in the middle of another controversy, when Stewart, who consulted the *Telegram* editors on how the city should be run, arranged for one of the judges to vote with him for Draper's dismissal. The judge happened to be a trustee of the *Telegram*, under the will of the paper's founder, John Ross Robertson, who had left the *Tely*'s profits to the Hospital for Sick Children. The other judge was known to be a strong Draper man. The plan was for Stewart to move a motion calling for the police chief's resignation, which would be seconded by the *Tely*'s judge.

The newspapers were tipped off that it would be doomsday for Draper.

At the *Star*, a senior reporter wrote the story in advance. A banner headline was prepared and the story set in type, ready to be used as soon as the vote was recorded. I was sent to the police commission meeting to phone in a confirmation of the result.

At the meeting, though, Mayor Stewart's hand went up alone. He turned to the judge, who was supposed to be on his side, and saw him raise his hand to vote with Draper's man against the dismissal motion. When I called the *Star* with the news, they wouldn't believe me and had somebody from the office phone Palmer Kent, the commission's secretary, to double-check what I had said.

Reporters were later told that Draper had been tipped off and had phoned some of his business friends. They were widely reported to have called Ottawa, and the *Tely*'s judge got a call, telling him that if he wanted to stay in good with the people who counted, he was to stay with Draper. It was a rare lapse of the *Tely*'s influence. In those days, if you weren't on the *Telegram* slate, you didn't get elected. It was the predominant paper in Toronto, while the *Star* was said to have the biggest circulation and the least influence. The *Telegram* once ran its own city editor for mayor and got him elected. That was Major Bert Wemp. He was such a poor mayor, the *Tely* didn't endorse him for a second term. He lost and went back to the paper as the women's editor.

Whenever I ran into Draper over the years, I was always left with the impression that he didn't fully understand what was going on. Following the Dorland case, the vacancy created by the removal of the chief of detectives was remedied by James C. McRuer, a top criminal lawyer and a special prosecutor in murder cases. He had the four top sergeants of detectives write an exam he had devised. John Chisholm's mark was far ahead of the others'. He became the chief of detectives and was soon recognized as the real brains of the force.

7

Red Ryan

THE OLD SOLDIERS, veterans of the First World War, liked Draper, who helped many of them with monetary assistance during the Depression. To his credit, if he had faith that they would go straight, he also used his influence with the business community to find jobs for men who had been released from jail.

He had absolutely no faith in Norman (Red) Ryan, Canada's most famous convict. This was in 1935, when Prime Minister R. B. Bennett, several senators, church leaders and others were working to have Ryan paroled from a life sentence in Kingston Penitentiary. The rehabilitation of criminals had become a popular cause, coupled with a widespread misconception that a lot of ex-convicts went back to jail because the cops began hounding them as soon as they were free and never gave them a chance to go straight. Draper and his deputy chief, George Guthrie, wrote to the remissions branch, warning that they were making a mistake about Ryan. Nevertheless, he was turned loose with the blessing of Father W. T. Kingsley of Kingston's Church of the Good Thief.

Canada's model ex-convict, as he was now known, returned to Toronto, his hometown, in a blare of publicity. The *Star* began a series of crime-doesn't-pay columns and stories under his name, ghost-written by Roy Greenaway, the paper's ace reporter, and Athol Gow. The Golden Boy of

Crime was even the guest of honor at that summer's police field day.

What people didn't know was that Ryan had almost immediately hooked up with some old buddies from his earlier penitentiary days. Within ten months of his release, he was to be shot dead by police bullets after killing a Sarnia, Ontario, police officer in a liquor store holdup.

The adulation that Ryan received wherever he went brings to mind a framed picture of him that I have. It was taken at the police field day. Ryan is standing with a judge, the chief coroner, a city controller, a prominent lawyer and the man who was in charge of the track meet. Ryan looks every bit as distinguished as the others. I've often shown the photo to people unacquainted with him and asked them to pick which of the six was the famous criminal. They usually choose someone other than Ryan. I don't blame them. If I hadn't met Ryan, I wouldn't have known which was the face of a vicious criminal. It belied his nature.

My opportunity to meet Ryan, whose name I had heard at school from older boys, including my brother Dave, came one night in July 1935, not long after he was released. A man walked into the press room at police headquarters and said he was to meet Athol Gow there. He was well dressed, mannerly and on the shy side. "I'm Red Ryan," he said, and I guessed he had come to see about the stories Gow and Greenaway were writing. Gow had known Ryan from his boyhood days in the same district of west-end Toronto. Gow, however, grew up to be a well-respected reporter, after starting as an office boy at the *Star*. Ryan ended up a bank robber and killer.

I had been speaking to him only a few minutes, when the police radio squawked out that there was a two-alarm fire at the Kedall Coal Yard up on Dupont Street. I said, "Jeez, I'll have to go, Red, but you stay here and wait for Athol."

"Can I go with you?" he asked. "I haven't seen a big fire in years."

I said, "I guess not, Red. Not since the big one you had down in Kingston."

I was referring to the huge fire he and other prisoners had set in 1923, when they staged a mass escape over the penitentiary walls and instigated an Ontario-wide crime wave. Ryan was free for three months before being recaptured. He just laughed at my remark and said, "Sure," and we raced out to the car.

It was often difficult for a reporter who wasn't generally known to get through fire lines. But when I approached the burning coal yard with Ryan that night, the fire line parted amid a flurry of handshakes from the police, who recognized my distinguished guest. It was like the arrival of a war hero. People clamored for his autograph, and the fire chief threw his arms around Red and led him close to the roaring flames, while a police sergeant bellowed at me to get away.

Back at headquarters an hour later, I shook hands with Ryan and left him in the office. His palm, I had noticed, was sweaty. It crossed my mind at the time that people with sweaty palms should not trusted, but I thought nothing more about it. Only later did I learn that just a couple of nights before Red and I visited the fire, a Stouffville village councillor, who also ran an auto agency, had been shot to death while he and his son were trying to prevent the theft of a new car, wanted by Ryan's gang for robbing banks in western Ontario. After Ryan was killed in Sarnia, ballistics tests of the gun he had used to kill the policeman showed it was the same one that had killed the car dealer. The dealer's son was severely wounded in the encounter and never fully recovered.

Ryan didn't need to rob to get money. At that time, when a job was next to impossible to get, he held two. He was night manager of a beverage room in Cabbagetown, which drew a full house every evening to see the model ex-convict going from table to table shaking hands. His other job was selling cars for a dealer in Weston. He got a salary plus a commission on sales. And his newspaper stories were bringing in money, too.

Before Ryan was killed, Pat Hogan, a Toronto police inspector, got a tip that he was meeting other ex-convicts, namely his buddies Harry Checkley and Ed (Wyoming) Mc-

Mullen. Checkley was killed with Ryan in Sarnia, and Mc-Mullen was later shot to death after he killed a customs man at the U.S. border near Vancouver.

Hogan also heard that Ryan had bought a Sherbourne Street prostitute a $4,000 mink coat, the very best on the 1936 market. But the police dared not try to tail him for fear of being accused of harassing a reformed con. So Ryan went his merry way, daily dyeing his red hair to mask his criminal doings. After the Sarnia killings, it was the next day before police were positive that the man on the morgue slab was the criminal who was supposed to be Canada's role model of rehabilitation.

Father Kingsley of the Church of the Good Thief was devastated by Ryan's return to crime and suffered a stroke. He died before the year was out, from what his colleagues said was a broken heart. Ryan's fall was hard for the public to swallow, and convicts said he set back parole at least twenty years.

From a personal perspective, by 1935 I had come a long way from the innocent boy in knickerbockers who had begun his training as a reporter only a few years earlier. But for a long time after my appointment as night police reporter, I still had to go into the *Star* in the morning and put out the children's page. As that bellowing police sergeant at the burning coal yard demonstrated, I still had a fair way to go.

In fact, the sergeant was not the only one to bellow at me in 1935. One day, I also received an astonishing tirade from C. L. Burton, the president of Simpsons and one of the most distinguished men in Toronto. The Harry H. Stevens committee in Ottawa had been holding hearings on prices, and the big merchants had come under a lot of fire. I happened to be at the *Star* on the morning the committee's report, which was very critical of Simpsons, was released. Word came that Burton was at the Royal York Hotel, and I was sent to get a comment from him.

In those days, Eaton's and Simpsons were so powerful that each had a police detective assigned to its big store. They were also such huge advertisers that we never reported anything that happened on their premises. We simply said the incident had occurred "in a downtown store." Nevertheless, the *Star* had been giving the Stevens committee wide coverage.

In front of the Royal York, a chauffeur told me that he was waiting for Burton, and I leaned against the wall and waited, too. When Burton emerged from the hotel, I identified myself and asked his opinion of the report. I didn't get any such thing. He began shouting and screaming his opinion of me, the Red *Star* of King Street West and the Communist bastards who worked there. A crowd gathered as every swear word in the book poured out of his mouth, along with a threat to punch me in the face if I didn't get out of his way. He might have done it, too, but the doorman and the chauffeur finally got him into the limousine and he was driven away, thus ending one of the biggest embarrassments I ever suffered as a young reporter.

On a more personal, positive note, 1935 was also the year that Marjorie and I married and went to live in an apartment in the Parkdale district. Our son, Ron, was born in February 1937. People have asked me why we didn't have more than one child. I've always said, "Listen, in the Depression, when your child was born in the hospital, you couldn't get him out until you'd paid the bill. I can still remember hustling up enough money to pay the private patients pavilion so my son could be released."

8

Thousands Thought an Innocent Man Was Hanged

IN 1936 I WAS SENT TO WATCH outside the Don Jail in east-end Toronto the night Harry O'Donnell was hanged for the sex murder of Ruth Taylor, a secretary who had been on her way home to the Beaches area from the downtown trust firm where she worked.

O'Donnell's trial was probably the first in Canada to feature forensic testimony. The prosecution argued that rabbit hair wool from the young woman's sweater had been found on O'Donnell's clothing. The forensics were the work of Professor L. Joslyn Rogers, the head of chemistry at the University of Toronto, which was almost directly across the street from headquarters. Professor Rogers loved to read Sherlock Holmes stories, and had helped the police on several cases. One time, I dropped into his lab to find him boiling a suspected murder victim's stomach, in search of a poison. He used a microscope to find the tiny strands of wool from Ruth Taylor's sweater.

O'Donnell was a motor mechanic who lived in the area of the murder and had previously come under police suspicion for sexually molesting women. His alibi was that at about the time Ruth Taylor was dragged into a ravine, raped and killed, he had been at the bedside of his wife, who had just given birth at a maternity home. The story stood up until police went over every foot of ground at the murder scene and discovered a wrench with the letters OD scratched on it. Did that mean the wrench was O'Donnell's?

At the trial, his counsel, Frank Regan, one of the top criminal lawyers of the time, called a self-styled criminologist as an expert witness. This was a man who, I always thought, would say anything for money. He told the court that he knew about tools and said OD meant outside dimensions. The Crown called witnesses from the toolmaking business, who said they had never heard of such a thing and that motor mechanics marked their tools to keep track of them in the garage. That and the evidence of the wool fibers convinced the jury that O'Donnell was guilty.

Frank Regan insisted that an innocent man was going to his death. The conviction was upheld on appeal, but petitions were taken up in many parts of the city and thousands of people signed in the belief that O'Donnell hadn't committed the murder. Women wept outside the jail the night he was hanged.

This widespread belief in his innocence was largely a creation of the *Star*. It happened this way. After O'Donnell was arrested, the paper learned that his wife was still in serious condition after childbirth and that she got the *Star* every night at supper. She had not been told that her husband had been charged with rape and murder because doctors feared that the news would kill her. The *Star* responded by printing a single copy of the paper containing no reference to the arrest, and this was delivered to her bedside. The regular editions of the paper headlined Harry O'Donnell's arrest and carried a boxed story on the front page telling about the single copy that had been printed to save the suspect's wife from possibly dying of shock.

A couple of days went by and Mrs. O'Donnell's condition improved enough for the doctors to break the news to her. She collapsed. The single copy earned the *Star* continent-wide publicity, as well as an award from the *Christian Science*

Monitor and praise from *Time* magazine for the compassion it showed when O'Donnell was charged.

The single-copy business alone would not have had that much effect on public opinion. But Frank Regan skillfully exploited it. During the trial, his defense strongly implied that this was a frame-up, that the strands from Ruth Taylor's sweater had been planted on O'Donnell's suit. He also planted stories about his client's innocence in the papers, which he was able to do because he had many friends who were newsmen, especially Major Claud Pascoe of the *Star*. The stories were read and believed by the public, and an angry crowd of two or three thousand gathered outside the Don Jail on the night of the execution.

This was the first hanging at which a newspaperman was not present. The managing editor of the *Mail and Empire*, who could no longer bear to assign his people to watch a man being put to death, had petitioned the Ontario government to ban the practice of using us as official witnesses at executions. I was glad he had. In my early *Star* days, I had seen a reporter return shaking from the jail one morning after witnessing the execution of a man named Stewart, and I certainly didn't want to watch a man die.

The crowd outside the Don Jail was very unruly, screaming and yelling its belief that Harry O'Donnell was innocent. However, there was nothing they could do about it, except wait for the official notice of the execution, signed by the chief coroner and the sheriff, to be tacked to the front door. When that was done, most of the people left, but many still lingered, and eventually the police chased them down through Riverdale Park, arresting some for vagrancy.

Belief in O'Donnell's innocence persisted until one newspaper reporter's concern finally put the matter to rest and earned him a big scoop. That was Doug Oliver, the *Mail and Empire*'s man at Queen's Park. One day, while talking to Attorney General Arthur Roebuck, he mentioned that he couldn't sleep some nights, wondering if an innocent man had been hanged. Roebuck wheeled around in his chair, opened the safe behind him and produced a statement signed by O'Donnell.

It was a confession to Ruth Taylor's murder. Not only that, but O'Donnell had confessed to climbing through windows in east-end Toronto and raping several other women. Some of these attacks had been reported to the area police station, but they had been dismissed as imagination or sexual trysts with boyfriends. Other rapes had never been reported, so only O'Donnell and the victims could have known about them. Frank Regan had a copy of the confession, too, but he had chosen to keep the public's belief in his client's innocence alive. Thus, Regan's good friend Claud Pascoe was scooped by Doug Oliver.

In the days when the death penalty was carried out, murder trials were dramatic things, and I never really got used to them. When it came time for the jury to come in with the verdict, I might as well have been the prisoner, I was so shaken. Hearing the judge utter the death sentence used to upset me something terrible, though I didn't show it because I didn't want to be seen feeling sorry for the prisoner. I was a police reporter. I worked with police, and *they* weren't sorry for the guy.

However, it was quite evident to me in those days that even in murder trials, where a man's life was at stake, there was still a law for the rich and a law for the poor. If you didn't have any money, you didn't have much defense. For instance, the Crown could call the very best psychiatric evidence, which they paid for. Defendants could rarely afford their own psychiatrists. Thus, the Crown's psychiatrist, usually from one of the big institutions, would sit in the courtroom throughout a trial. Then, at the end, he would take the stand and testify without any risk of contradiction that he had observed the defendant closely and come to the conclusion that he was sane.

The most outrageous abuse of this procedure I ever saw was in Napanee, Ontario, in the late forties, at the conclusion of what I had called the Human Target case. The Crown's psychiatrist duly testified that the defendant, a boy who had killed two people, was absolutely sane, and the court accepted his opinion without question. But that psychiatrist was staying at the same hotel I was, and I had heard him screaming through the night with the DTs.

I'm not saying innocent people were hanged. But I often felt sorry for the person who was found guilty, because in some cases I could see he hadn't received a really good defense. Harry O'Donnell, though, got a vigorous defense and was not wrongly hanged.

9

City of Bookies

FOR YEARS, THE NEWSPAPERS RAN regular editorials about how clean Toronto was and how the pure civic air was never disturbed by a breath of scandal. It sounded good, but those editorials tended to be written by people who had no idea what was really going on.

In the thirties and early forties, for example, there was a *Tely* reporter at city hall who could get you anything, including a dog license, at half price. He could even get a summons quashed for half the cost of the expected fine. We knew, but could never prove, that prominent people charged with drunken driving received private, unrecorded hearings in magistrates' offices. Today such doings would be front-page scandals, but back then they and many other things went on as a matter of course in what civic boosters liked to refer to as "the city of churches." It would have been just as accurate to call Toronto a city of bookie joints.

In an earlier chapter, I mentioned that I bought my Ford roadster with the proceeds of a tip on a crooked horse race. The tip came from a bookie. I had become a horse player during my copy boy days, when one of my duties involved sitting by the ticker tape machine in the composing room, compiling baseball scores and race results.

In the old Hollywood newspaper movies, the hero or somebody always screams *"Stop the presses!"* when a major story breaks. At the *Star*, the only thing the presses ever stopped for was the very latest baseball scores, which were punched, inning by inning, onto the printing plates by hand. The *Star* and the *Evening Telegram* each had a large scoreboard running across the top of the front page. Most ball games were played in the afternoon, and if the *Tely* had a final score that we didn't, the copy boy responsible had to explain in writing why we had been scooped. Usually the reason was that Scotty Davey, the superintendent of the press room and father of the future senator Keith Davey, had decided that they were behind in the run and refused to stop, even if you screamed at him.

The printers liked to look at the race results on the ticker tape, and I began placing bets for them with a bookie I knew. It was a little sideline, earning me a small commission, and I kept it up through my early days as a reporter.

In 1936, Lou Marsh, the *Star*'s sports editor, somehow got hold of a list of downtown bookie joints that the police never raided. They were all in one particular division, and the implication was that the divisional inspector was being paid off. Since I knew bookies and went to the track all the time, I was temporarily taken off the night police beat and put on the story with Barney Armstrong, a disbarred lawyer who was working as a reporter. I was given Marsh's list and sent out to place bets at the protected bookie joints, most of which were run by a guy called Manny Feder, the king of the bookmakers in Toronto. The word was that each week he sent out a man named Pinky with an envelope for the police. I never saw the envelope, but I did see Pinky go into the police station a number of times.

There were an awful lot of places downtown where you could bet, many with loudspeakers broadcasting running accounts of the races out onto the sidewalk. Queen Street in particular was rife with the joints, and one of them was right across from city hall. It was above Bowles' Restaurant, run by a man named Playfair Brown, who was a boxing promoter and the superintendent of an Anglican Sunday school.

Farther along Queen Street, I encountered an exasperated bookie barber, who was next door to a loudspeaker-equipped shop. "Lookit," he said to me, "I keep getting raided by the cops, and this guy, he keeps going. He broadcasts right out on the street and he never gets raided." As Barney and I reported in our stories, it was the same throughout the division — the cops regularly raided some places, while they completely ignored others.

The assignment got kind of risky after the first article appeared and the bookies became suspicious of strangers who were putting up bets. I got some dirty looks, but nobody caught on, and I had a couple of good days, the best one being when I bet on a horse called Marge that paid the limit — fifteen to one. As we duly reported in one of the stories, all winnings were contributed to the *Star*'s Fresh Air Fund.

For the first couple of days, Chief Draper ignored our reports. He thought it was just the *Star* trying to get at him again. But the politicians were being asked what was going on, especially in this gambling joint right across the street from city hall. That place and others were raided. Then things got hot, and Draper promised a big investigation. At the *Star*, someone realized that if Barney Armstrong's shady past came out in this heated climate, it could be very embarrassing for the paper. So they took him off the story and assigned Roy Greenaway to work with me. Barney later became our Ottawa man and a close friend of Mackenzie King.

As far as hard evidence of police protection went, we never got too much beyond the obvious implications of the fact that until our stories appeared, there were bookie joints that didn't get raided. For his part, Draper refused to believe that the inspector in question, whom he described as one of his most loyal men, was crooked. Draper probably would have taken no action at all on his own, but he got the word from his political masters, and the inspector was transferred to another division.

The *Star* did not go on another antigambling crusade until 1938. I was in on that, too, because by then I had been transferred from the night beat and was working out of headquarters as the junior day police reporter. The senior man was still Athol Gow.

With the exception of that one particular division, the Toronto police were pretty clean and worked hard to keep the gamblers in check. One time, they even raided the *Canadian Racing Form* after getting a Crown attorney's opinion that the paper was illegally disseminating betting information. But the bookie joints were really small potatoes. The heavy action was at the magnificent gambling casinos that operated openly in the townships just outside Toronto, where the police forces were very small.

As far back as I could remember, the National Sporting Club had nightly played host to a select clientele at its well-guarded spot on Lakeshore Boulevard West, just past the city limits. It was run by Abe Orpen, owner of Dufferin Race Track in Toronto and the Long Branch track in what is now Etobicoke. Occasionally there was a token raid on the National, with a nominal fine imposed, but never anything that got much more than a couple of paragraphs in the papers.

Orpen had some very good friends in Toronto political circles and on the police force and at the newspapers. Top men in the sports departments worked as handsomely paid stewards and judges at his race tracks. Many of the men working the mutuels machines, selling and cashing tickets, were reporters, as well, including a couple who covered the court beat. At the Dufferin track, there was a special hospitality room for politicians and newsmen, and some cops used to say that being friends with Abe Orpen could help you get a promotion.

His sedate, exclusive National Club operated more or less quietly for years and had all the business to itself. Then Manny Feder opened a couple of clubs, the Combine and the Brown Derby, both on Lakeshore Boulevard. In what is now Mississauga, Bill Beasley opened the plush Brookwood Club, where the male clientele often arrived in top hats and tails. In East York, a man named Dave Garrity established the Todmorden Club at Broadview Avenue and Pottery Road. And there was another East York club, known as the Potato Warehouse. I don't know who ran that one, but it had some extra scandal attached to it: how were the gamblers able to get a permit to build a potato warehouse without somebody from East York Township going to see if it *was* a potato warehouse?

Most of the clubs were small versions of the Las Vegas casinos, with gambling games and chalkboards showing the results and prices at horse racing parks all over the U.S. Running accounts of the races by the track callers came over loudspeakers direct from the parks. As newspapermen, we all knew about the clubs and visited them often, mainly because you could get all you wanted to eat and drink for nothing. Late in the evening, we would jump into the car and drop by the Todmorden Club or one of the others and have a few sandwiches and, if we had an extra fifty cents, play a game of blackjack. One night, I threw down my last fifty cents and ended up winning twenty-one dollars. That was more than I made in a week.

As the clubs gained in popularity, there were incessant complaints to police and newspapers, but nothing was done. The newspapers weren't crusading. And word got around that the casino operators had nothing to fear, because they were big contributors to the provincial Liberal party. Anyway, Premier Mitchell F. Hepburn was too busy battling American labor unions, which he had vowed to keep out of the province, to be interested in fighting casino owners. Toronto police sources told us that Lionel Conacher, the MPP for Brackendale, was the bagman responsible for collecting the gamblers' payoffs.

The clubs lasted until 1938, when the Reverend Gordon Domm, a popular, spellbinding orator, attacked them in a series of sermons from his pulpit at Bathurst Street United Church. Why, Domm demanded to know, were the police taking no action, when wives were complaining that their husbands were losing their entire pay in these places? The Reverend Domm, whose son, William, is now an MP and a prominent advocate of capital punishment, sent copies of the sermons to Joseph E. Atkinson, the publisher of the *Star*, who ordered them printed on the front page every Monday.

The sermons stung the attorney general into action. The Toronto police and the OPP formed a joint squad and smashed their way into most of the clubs. I was one of the reporters taken on the raids of the Brown Derby, the Combine and other places. We were told nothing in advance. On the night of a raid, we were simply advised to stick around headquarters because something was going to happen. Then, when the squad got to a club, they would call back and say, "Okay, we're here," and we would race out to the scene with our cameramen. The police wanted publicity, so we were usually in time to get pictures of the prisoners being escorted out and put into the wagon.

At the Potato Warehouse, Arthur Van of the *Telegram* put his camera up to take a man's picture and the guy ran at him and broke his nose and kicked the camera to smithereens. The guy was charged with assault, and in court the next day, he had a check already written out to replace the camera.

For the Brown Derby raid, which was actually my first visit to that club, I took an artist along to make sketches of what it looked like inside. The police showed us through the building and pointed out an escape tunnel, which they had known about ahead of time. They said they had found $1,400, which someone had dropped on the floor of the tunnel while trying to get away. Manny Feder wasn't in his office when the cops sledgehammered their way into it, but they nabbed him a while later, trying to sneak out a side door of the Royal York Hotel, where he maintained a suite.

The police had a warrant to search the suite, and as they were walking Feder back to it, he dropped a key. It fit a safety deposit box in the hotel's vault and unlocked the secret of the large crap table losses that gamblers had suffered at the Derby and the Combine. For years, Manny had enjoyed a reputation as an honest casino owner, but his box contained dozens of dice, all cleverly loaded against turning up sevens or elevens.

The National Club, which had never been as wide open as the others, was not raided. Orpen quietly closed it on his own. There were, however, stories that the club was reopened just as quietly after the heat was off.

These days, you almost never hear about gambling raids. Probably one reason is that the police are too busy with crack, cocaine and heroin. And people can do a lot of legal gambling now. Lotto 6/49, for example, is really just the government's version of what, in my day, used to be known as the numbers racket.

10

The Murder of Jimmy Windsor

EARLY IN JANUARY 1939, Toronto residents were shocked to read newspaper headlines that the city had had its first gangland killing.

That was how the murder of bookmaker Jimmy Windsor was presented to the public by all three dailies. The way the gang of four men had invaded Windsor's Briar Hill Avenue home, and the way he had been shot while having supper with his two sisters, their husbands and his eighteen-year-old girlfriend, had the unmistakable ring of an underworld killing.

Windsor died on the kitchen floor with two detectives crouched beside him, asking, "Who shot you?" Obviously, he didn't know. All he said was the word "doctor," repeating it a couple of times before he took his last breath. The five witnesses told the detectives that the men had robbed Windsor of a roll of bills and some jewelry, and the man who shot him had also kicked him several times.

I was the first reporter to arrive at Windsor's house. I was on weekend duty and had been at home, eating my own supper with an ear on our radio, which could somehow pick up the one-way police calls. There were no two-way radios in police cars then. Briar Hill Avenue was hardly more than a mile away.

The first detective to come out of the house whispered to me that Windsor was no great loss. He was a bookmaker with a gang of runners who picked up bets in downtown stores and factories for a ten percent commission. I had never heard of him. He had probably owed someone a lot of money, the detective guessed.

I talked to the neighbors, said the police had told me that Windsor was a bookmaker downtown, and a man from two doors along said, "Well, I don't know about being a book-maker, but I know he runs a night club up on Yonge Street, up at Lansing there."

Lansing was in the suburbs then, at Sheppard Avenue. Windsor's club was actually a dime-a-dance hall. Those places were sometimes associated with rough characters and hoodlums, and the neighbor figured the murder had something to do with the dance hall.

The gangland atmosphere increased when the police brought the five witnesses out to the cars, taking them down to headquarters to look at mug shots. That was standard procedure in homicide cases in those days. But these witnesses came out with their faces covered. And not just with paper bags or newspaper. They had cloths wrapped around their noses and lower parts of their faces, which gave me the idea that the police really figured this must be a gangland thing.

The truth was, at that point they had no idea why Windsor had been killed or who might have done it. At headquarters, though, the whole detective squad was called in and ordered to go out and show some activity.

To show some activity in those days, the cops went out and rounded up some of the criminals they knew. The usual suspects. In this case, the witnesses had described two of the gang as looking like Italians, so it was a bad night for criminals with Italian names and dark complexions. By then I was at headquarters with a photographer, who banged pictures of the steady stream of police and their swarthy prisoners emerging from the elevator. At one point I asked a detective why he had brought a particular rounder in, and he said, "We have to bring in somebody, so I brought him."

The rounder's photo was on the front page of the *Star* the next day.

The activity pleased Chief Draper, who had come in and was down in his office. He liked the newspapers to say he was personally in charge of a case, and he was often on hand when his men made an important arrest. After the charge was laid, the procedure was for the suspect to be paraded in front of the chief, and many a prisoner was utterly unnerved by Draper's wrath. In one case, a man who had been released from the penitentiary after serving a term for raping a child in a park in Rosedale, the area where Toronto's elite lived, repeated the offense in the same neighborhood. When the man was brought before him, Draper produced an army sword from a cupboard and convinced the guy that he was about to have his penis cut off piece by piece. When he was finally taken to the cells, the prisoner had to be supported by two detectives.

In the Windsor case, Draper didn't call the press in until the next day. By then the detectives had established that their rounders knew nothing about the murder. All but two were let go. The two couldn't or wouldn't offer an alibi, and they were remanded a week in the Don Jail under the catch-all vagrancy charge that doesn't exist in the Criminal Code today.

At his press conference, Draper told us what a disservice to the public we would be doing if we printed the pictures of the witnesses that our papers had been rounding up. The witnesses' lives were at stake, Draper said. The papers paid no attention to him and ran the photos, anyway.

At the *Star*, a night editor named Dave Griffin played up the gangland angle, taking my report and several others and combining them into a story with a lead about a machine-gun gang killing Jimmy Windsor on Saturday night. Windsor had been shot with a pistol. The machine gun was Dave's inspiration.

All the newspapers carried stories suggesting that a protection racket, or an attempt by one gang of gamblers to take over another gang's territory, was behind the killing. An editorial in the *Star* said gangland warfare was invading the city from New York and the police had better get busy and clean it up. The scores of bookies who operated in just about every other barber shop and variety store in Toronto became alarmed, fearful that the gang that had killed Windsor would come after them next. Some had actually been held up by four men before the murder, but hadn't reported it out of a natural reluctance to discuss their business with the police.

The police still seemed unable to figure out why Windsor, who had offered no resistance to the holdup men, had been killed, and the headlines continued. At the *Star*, Dave Griffin convinced the city editor that the killing was probably the work of the Black Hand, as the Mafia was then called. The Ontario Black Hand was centered in Hamilton, with Rocco Perri, the self-styled king of the bootleggers, its godfather. His wife, Bessie, had been gunned down behind their home by rival mobsters. Griffin had once worked in Hamilton and had good connections there, so he was sent to dig up a link between the Perri mob and the attempt to take over the Toronto bookmakers.

In those days, an out-of-town assignment at the paper's expense was a rare treat for an overworked, poorly paid newsman. From what Dave told me later, I gathered that when he got off the bus in Hamilton, he went straight to his favorite bootlegging joint and rarely emerged, except once an evening, to go to the telegraph office and send a story to the *Star*.

The first one quoted police as saying they had the Windsor killers bottled up in the Niagara Peninsula. Each succeeding story carried a different dateline, creating the impression that the police cordon was gradually closing in on Niagara Falls, and that there would be a big shoot-out when the gang was finally cornered at the border. The final story said the killers had given police the slip, and Dave returned to Toronto.

The Toronto police were not displeased by the stories. Keeping a crime alive on the front page is often the best way to get people coming forward with information. With interest in the Windsor killing so high, the police were able to get the

provincial government to offer a $1,000 reward for the cap-
ture and conviction of the killers, and this was added to the
$500 that the city council and the Toronto Police Commis-
sion had each put up. Two thousand dollars was enough to
get underworld tongues wagging. Ironically, the rewards of
$50,000 and $100,000 posted in modern-day murder cases
have never solved a single crime, in my memory.

As for the *Star*, Dave Griffin's adventures in Hamilton were
all part of what we called "making the news." You were never
ordered to make the news, but it was implied that you did it
anyhow, and no one bothered to challenge you on it. You just
had to be careful about libel and slander.

I had nothing more to do with the Windsor case, until the
Tely scooped us some months later.

My friend Sid Hibbs was covering the courts, and a
rounder that he knew, who had just been bailed out of the
Don Jail, told him that a prisoner there named Mickey Mac-
Donald was sounding off about how the cops were trying to
frame him for the Windsor murder and were going to charge
him. Sid passed the tip on to the *Tely*'s day police reporter,
and the paper ran a big headline story that a prisoner in the
Don Jail was a prime suspect in the Windsor case. MacDonald's name was not used.

Athol Gow wasn't around that day, so I took the call from
the office, demanding to know why *we* hadn't got the story.
The thing was, I *did* have the story, and I knew a hell of a lot
more than the *Tely* did. A senior detective had told me that
Mickey's brother, Alex MacDonald, and a man named John
Shea had been charged with a bank robbery up in Brampton.
Shea had then approached the police and offered to tell
them what had happened to Jimmy Windsor if the robbery
charge was dropped. A deal was made, and Shea told how
he, Mickey, Alex and a Louis Gallo had gone to Windsor's
house to rob him. Only Alex and Mickey, who was very
drunk, were armed, and Mickey shot Windsor for speaking to
him sarcastically.

The senior detective had told me all this in confidence,
with my promise not to write anything until a charge was
laid. But, smarting from that rocket from the office, and the

fact that I had been scooped on something I knew all about, I sat down in a fit of temper and wrote the story. I named names, included all the details and completely deflated the *Tely*'s scoop.

The police, particularly John Chisholm, the chief of detectives, were furious. So was Cecil L. Snyder, the prosecutor who had been working on the case. Not only had I betrayed a confidence, they steamed, I had also warned MacDonald that one of his confederates was going to testify against him. Shea's life was now in danger!

I didn't buy that last bit. MacDonald, who was in jail for a liquor truck hijacking, must have heard about the deal before my story appeared. Otherwise, how come he was mouthing off about a frame-up? But there was no use arguing with them, and it was some time before I was forgiven.

Mickey and Alex MacDonald's trial was held early in 1940. Cecil L. Snyder was probably the best criminal prosecutor Ontario ever had. He lost only one of the twenty-eight murder cases he tried. Frank Regan, the late Harry O'Donnell's counsel, defended the brothers. I was put on the story after the jury had retired, which meant waiting around until they brought back a verdict.

The city hall press room looked like a scene from *The Front Page*, with the reporters sitting around, playing cribbage and gossiping and taking the odd shot from a crock of Wiser's Special Blend, our drink of choice in those days. Among the reporters was young John Bassett, who was working for the *Globe*. He would later buy the *Telegram* and preside over the climax of its rivalry with the *Star*.

Also waiting in the room was Mickey's wife, Kitty Kat MacDonald, a good-looking but rather hard-boiled girl in her early twenties, a few years younger than her husband. She was always beautifully dressed, and on that day she wore a silver fox fur around her neck.

Kitty had had a few drinks, too, and took a shine to young Bassett. She sidled around to where he was playing cribbage, got as close to him as she possibly could and flicked the fur at him, saying, "Here, big boy, play with some tail." Poor John's face went completely red. I remember that as clearly as I do the sheriff's officer running into the room about eleven p.m. and saying the jury was coming back.

They had found Mickey guilty, and he was sentenced to hang. Snyder seemed to have won another one. But about that time, a young lawyer named Goldwyn Arthur Martin was making a name for himself in the Ontario Court of Appeal, bringing up legal points that had never been heard before and winning new trials for his clients. He did that for Mickey MacDonald. Then, at the second trial, Martin cast doubt on the validity of Shea's story, given the deal he had made with the prosecution, and the killer was acquitted.

So MacDonald beat his date with the hangman. However, he still had to stand trial for hijacking the liquor truck and was sent to Kingston for fourteen years.

In the summer of 1947, Mickey, a prominent bank robber named Ulysses Lauzon and a petty crook called Nick Minelli escaped from their cells in a way that raised hints of collusion with penitentiary guards. The internal investigation that followed failed to discover why no one had seen anything amiss the night the trio went down the long rope. Nor did the investigators learn where the rope and other tools needed for the breakout had come from.

Lauzon and MacDonald staged a $40,000 bank robbery in Windsor and fled across the border. Years went by without any more being heard from them. Then a decomposed body that was identified as Lauzon's was found in a swamp near Pascagoula, Mississippi. The police assumed that Mickey MacDonald had ended his days there, too. The family name was kept alive by his young brother, Edwin, who also became one of G. A. Martin's clients.

11

Scooped by the Censors

IN TELLING THE STORY OF JIMMY WINDSOR and the capture of his killers, I have got a bit ahead of myself. The Windsor story broke in 1939, the same year Marjorie, Ron and I moved from the house we'd been renting on Cheston Road in North Toronto for $32 a month, into a house on Rumsey Road in Leaside. It cost $4,650, with a down payment of $400. If you paid $600, the builder threw in screens and storms for all the windows free. With houses in Leaside going for almost half a million dollars today, $4,650 may not sound like much, but at the time, my salary was only $30 a week.

In 1939, Toronto was still very much a bastion of the British Empire, and, as I've said, one of the reasons our paper was called the Red *Star* was that people resented the news from Russia that we ran, which was widely considered to be Communist propaganda. It was thought that if the news wasn't about the Empire, it was no good.

The "Red" epithet must have secretly stung Joseph E. Atkinson. At any rate, the money he spent on our coverage of the 1939 Royal Tour really only makes sense if it is seen at least in part as an attempt to prove that he and his paper were as loyal as anybody. He went absolutely all out, ordering mass coverage of the King and Queen everywhere they went. Accordingly, I was sent to cover a brief appearance in Parry Sound and a layover at a railway siding in South Parry Sound.

The only story to be had in Parry Sound was the disappointment of the people. The Royal Couple was to have come out onto the back of the train and waved as they passed through town, but they had spent too much time in a mine at Sudbury and were sleeping when the train sped past their waiting subjects. They were still sleeping in South Parry Sound, while the train was parked, as scheduled, on the siding. My job was simply to get a picture of the train and forward it to Toronto, which I did and thus ended my only Royal Tour coverage. I did not see the King and Queen when they came to Toronto. I was back at police headquarters. The city was supposed to be a hotbed of radicals, and the police and newsmen were ready for anything, but apart from a brick thrown on Wellington Street, the visit passed without a hitch.

In normal times, the Royal Tour would have been the top story of the year, but 1939 was also the year the Second World War began. We got a taste of it almost immediately, when the Germans sunk the *Athenia*, an ocean liner with a large number of passengers from Toronto. We worked two days without sleep, chasing around after the pictures of every local person who had been on that boat. And, almost immediately after that, I got my first big scoop of the war.

I did it simply by walking into Stoodleigh's Restaurant, on the ground floor of the *Star* building, at the right time. A woman sitting at the counter was excitedly pressing her neighbor, a man in the middle of his morning coffee and Danish, to call the police. She was clearly upset by the sight of another man at the counter, who was sitting near the cashier.

"And what should I tell the police?" the first man asked.

"Tell them there's a man from Berlin and I think he's a spy," the woman said.

The man gave her an off look, as though peering into her eyes for signs of mental imbalance. But the woman leaned close and whispered something to him and he hurried out to the *Star*'s reception area, where there was a phone.

Two policemen arrived about five minutes later, just as the second man, still unaware of the bustle at the other end of the counter, was wiping his mouth and getting ready to go. The woman told the police that she had met the man during a business trip to Berlin. They'd had dinner together, and he had told her that he worked for the government. The tone of his remarks had left her with no doubt that he was a fervent Nazi. It was clear from their faces that the cops doubted that the man was a spy. But their orders were that all such suspicions had to be checked out thoroughly, and suspected spies were to be detained for vetting by the special branches of the RCMP and Toronto police.

The police put the man and the woman into their car and took them to the Court Street station, about three blocks away. When I got there, everyone was in front of the station sergeant, and the woman was telling the man, "You know me well. We had dinner together in Berlin." But the man had produced some convincing identification, and although he spoke with a slight accent, the sergeant seemed inclined to let the guy go. In fact, when he realized that I was listening to what was going on, the sergeant turned to me and said, "There's nothing here. Call us later, and if there is anything, we'll let you know."

That was a stock response to nosy reporters. Often they did not let you know. So I hung around outside and was soon rewarded by the sight of two members (in fact, the only two members) of the Toronto police Red squad going into the station. Until the war, they had been solely concerned with the Communist party, which had been outlawed by the Criminal Code of Canada. Now they were hunting Nazis.

I got even more excited when a couple of RCMP Special Branch officers arrived. But, hours later, when the Mounties and the Toronto detectives left the building, they brushed past me without a word. The sergeant, however, was more cooperative. "They've got something good," he told me. "The woman was right."

What a story! Even though I didn't have the guy's name, I had heard he'd been detained under the War Measures Act, and it was quite clear that a major spy ring had been broken up, just as it was starting to operate. I put everything I could into the story and was looking forward to front-page headlines. But then I ran right into the biggest wartime cross that we reporters had to bear.

My scoop was sent over to the *Globe and Mail* building, where the official news censor, a former senior employee of that paper, had his office. Half an hour later, the story came back dead with the words DON'T USE stamped on it. Wartime censorship was, I suppose, a necessary evil, but it often got ridiculous and I doubt that the public ever realized how closely controlled the war news was, and how much they were never allowed to know.

For instance, several prominent Toronto people of German and Italian extraction were interned as soon as war broke out. They had often been mentioned in the papers, but now we were not allowed to print their names. Also, there were many independent breweries in those days, and each one had a German brewmaster. One morning they disappeared, and neither their families nor their employers had any idea where they had gone. The newspapers knew, but we were forbidden to inform our readers that almost all the brewmasters were members of the German Canadian Bund, and that squads of Mounties had been waiting for every one of them, whether they were members or not, when they arrived for work that day. Under the special powers given to the police, the internees' families did not have to be notified for forty-eight hours.

Censorship also prevented us from telling the public that some thirty thousand German prisoners of war had been quietly brought to secret camps in Canada. Some of the camps were in remote, sparsely populated areas of Northern Ontario, where there was the odd escape by an individual prisoner. Since the camps were secret, and there were few people in the neighborhood, the escapes were not mentioned, either, and the censors seemed to have everything under control. But, as we learned in 1940, they had clearly not given much thought to what the drill should be in the event of a mass escape in the densely populated south.

The farce came about this way. The Geneva Convention

stipulated that captured officers were to be maintained in appropriate style. Thus, the patients were taken away and a large number of German officers were lodged in a sanatorium on the shore of Lake Muskoka, near Gravenhurst and not far from the cottages of Toronto's elite. That summer, the Germans were the talk of the cottagers, who could not help but notice the crowd of young men frolicking in the water in front of the sanatorium as they cruised by in their boats. The prisoners were guarded by members of the Veterans Guard of Canada, First World War vets, who had very little love for the offspring of men who had been their mortal enemies a generation before. Many of them wondered if Allied prisoners had anything to match the Germans' luxurious accommodation.

Early in August, one of the *Star*'s stringers in the area reported that Gravenhurst was rife with rumors that there had been a mass breakout at the sanatorium. I was called around midnight and told to get up there with Gordon Sinclair and a photographer named Strathy Smith. It was a dreadful, rainy night, and when Strathy and I arrived at Sinclair's beautiful house near Burnhamthorpe Road in Islington, Gordon refused to go. He stepped outside, had a look at the weather and said, "They can go to hell. I'll go in the morning."

Although he was still the highest-paid member of the staff, Sinclair had been in the *Star*'s doghouse for quite some time. His travels around the world on behalf of the paper were legendary, but these trips had ended several years earlier and, for whatever reason, he had been overlooked as a war correspondent. The fact that he wasn't in England, writing about Canada's troops and how the Londoners were enduring the nightly air raids, I think, hurt his pride. He never did get to Gravenhurst, and soon after that left the *Star* and joined General Motors as a public relations man.

Anyway, Strathy and I went on alone and, the next morning, found that the guards at the sanatorium were under orders not to let newspapermen anywhere near the place. So we went to the beverage room of our hotel and got talking to some off-duty guards. I coaxed a couple up to my room, where there was plenty of free beer, and got them to tell their story, which wasn't too difficult because the guards were anxious to get across to the public that *they* hadn't screwed up. The prisoners had dug a long tunnel down to the lakeshore because the grounds leading to the roadway were well-covered by the guards. I've never found out how they managed to do it or how they got rid of the excavated earth, but we presumed it was somehow carted to the lake and disposed of there.

But of course nothing could be got across to the public because the censors were holding to the rule that the camps could not be mentioned, even now when any number of possibly dangerous Germans were running around loose in cottage country. The argument raged in Toronto and Ottawa, while we hung around town, trying everything to get into the sanatorium and see the commander, Colonel Bull, a member of the noted Bull family of Brampton. Percy Cole of the *Tely* came up with a plan that nearly got us through. He called his editor, Major Wemp, the former mayor, and said, "Bert, I want you to send me a wire saying, 'Please see Colonel Bull at once,' and sign it 'Major Wemp.'"

Wemp did, and when Percy and I arrived at the sanatorium gate, he showed the wire to the guard, who said, "Yes, sir," and respectfully let us pass. Colonel Bull, on the other hand, was neither respectful nor amused, and ordered a squad of rifle-toting guards to escort us the hell out of there.

The impasse broke when a top man from the Defense Department in Ottawa arrived in Gravenhurst and agreed that yes, the public should indeed be told about the escaped prisoners in their midst. The Army Provost Corps released photos of escapees, which were run in the papers. At Union Station, in Toronto, a citizen looked up from his newspaper and saw the escaped U-boat captain he had just been reading about waiting for a train. The police were called and Sergeant John Nimmo was sent to make the arrest. Nimmo, a colorful, high-profile detective, had served in the Royal Navy after the First World War, and he and his prisoner had a pleasant chat about sailing on the North Sea, while they posed for a photographer. It was, of course, a front-page picture, and it brought an immediate reprimand from Ottawa: it was a violation of the Geneva Convention to take pictures of prisoners for publication.

Up in the Muskoka area we had a merry old time, chasing along the back roads from lake to lake with the cops and the soldiers, following up tips from citizens. One cottager told me that a German with excellent English had told him that it wouldn't be long until "we control everything." The German, the cottager said, had detailed knowledge of the fall of France and the Low Countries, and a lot of it was information that hadn't been carried by the local papers and radio.

The mystery was solved by Defense Department investigators, who discovered that the Germans had built a powerful shortwave radio at the sanatorium. They had got the parts from their guards, telling them that they were building the set so they could listen to music. One of them had said he particularly liked the Emerson Gill Orchestra, which broadcast from the Trianon Ballroom in Cleveland over station WTAM. In truth, the Germans had built the radio to get in touch with Berlin.

The chase lasted a couple of weeks. The authorities never did say how many prisoners had escaped, but from the captures made in Muskoka and as far east as Montreal, we guessed that the number was over twenty. After the war, we learned that one of the fugitives, a pilot, did actually get back to Germany. He rejoined his unit and was again shot down, this time fatally.

One fugitive was captured in the Bala area and put in the small local jail. His cell overlooked the road and hundreds of holidayers gathered, clamoring for his autograph and snapping pictures. The police had no beef with people taking photos and did not interfere. But, as Strathy and I found out when we were ordered over to Huntsville to cover the capture of yet another fugitive, the military was taking the ban on pictures for publication very seriously indeed.

The Huntsville prisoner, who was not one of the Gravenhurst escapees, had actually been captured by a *Star* reporter named Norman Phillips. Norman had been covering an escape at a remote camp near Sudbury, and when most of the escapees had been caught, he had headed back to

Toronto in his car. Near Huntsville, he picked up a tired-looking hitchhiker who did not speak English very well. Realizing that the guy could very well be one of the fugitives, Norman made some excuse and dropped his passenger on a side road and raced into Huntsville, where the police were having a church parade, led by the chief.

Norman told a cop who was not in the parade that the man he'd just dropped off was probably an escaped POW. The cop said it would have to wait till the parade was over. But Norman, incensed by the cop's offhand manner, stepped into the street, caught up with the chief and explained the situation as they both marched along at the head of the parade. The chief told Norman that it was a serious offense to interfere with a religious parade and threatened to arrest him if he didn't get back on the sidewalk.

Fortunately the parade did not go on much longer, and the escapee was still trudging down the road when the police arrived. Since a *Star* man had, in effect, captured the guy, the office wanted a picture badly. Strathy got it just moments before an Army unit arrived to claim the prisoner. Someone told the captain about our photo and he strode toward Strathy, demanding that he hand over the camera. There was no *way* we could return to the office without the picture, so Strathy backed out of the officer's reach. I was already running. Strathy threw the camera. I caught it and kept on running.

It was a front-page picture.

12

Making the News in Cobourg

IN THE EARLY WAR YEARS, I covered two big stories in Cobourg, a small town on Lake Ontario, about sixty miles east of Toronto. One was the trial of Dennis C. Draper, Toronto's chief of police, which took place in 1941. The other was the sensational 1942 shotgun murder of a Toronto private detective and his female assistant.

The Draper story began one night when he was driving home after a visit with his friend, the chief of police in Peterborough, who was a notorious boozer. Near Cobourg, Draper's car veered into the next lane and collided with an oncoming automobile. When the local police arrived, they found the chief directing traffic around the site. There was liquor on his breath. A man who had been in the other car died a few days later, and Draper was charged with dangerous driving.

Of course all the Toronto papers sent reporters to Cobourg for Draper's trial, which was presided over by a judge who had been brought in from Lindsay. Draper was found guilty and fined $500. I still don't know how anyone, no matter who his friends are, can be convicted of a Criminal Code offense and keep his job as chief of police, but Draper did. The issue simply faded away, though it did pop up briefly at a police commission hearing I covered not long after the trial.

The matter in question was whether a certain man should be granted a restaurant license. Draper was vigorously opposed, but wouldn't say why. The man's lawyer, Eddie Murphy, insisted he either give the commission the reason or withdraw his opposition, but all Draper would say was, "Honorable Board, I don't want to say here why he shouldn't have the license." As he spoke, he looked pointedly at the press table, implying that his information was too delicate to be made public.

But Murphy kept calling for an explanation, and finally the commissioners said, "Well, if you don't tell us, Chief, we'll have to give the man his license."

"Well, he's not a fit and proper person to *have* a license," Draper blurted, hammering the table with his fist.

"But *why* is he not a fit and proper person?"

"Well, if you *must* know," Draper cried, "he's got a criminal record."

And with that, Eddie Murphy leaped to his feet and said, "But, Chief, don't *you* have a criminal record, too?"

Draper just glared at Murphy, as though trying to melt him with his eyes. The "criminal," it turned out, had served a heavy sentence for a jewelry store robbery in Buffalo many years earlier and had not been in trouble since. The commissioners didn't turn against Draper right then, but the guy got his license at a meeting two weeks later.

As for the shotgun slayings, the victims were William Wallace Cunningham, a flamboyant private detective who chain-smoked cigars, and Agnes Fardella, a Cobourg woman who worked with him. In those days, adultery and insanity were the only grounds for divorce, and it was common for private detectives to be hired to contrive adulterous situations. The usual drill was for the husband to go to a hotel room with a woman hired by the detective and shortly afterward, the detective would burst in and "discover" them there. The woman became the corespondent cited in the divorce action (thus keeping the name of the husband's actual lover out of the proceedings) and the detective could swear truthfully in court that he had indeed caught this man in adultery. There was never any mention that the man had probably paid the detective an awful lot of money to catch him.

Agnes Fardella was not a prostitute. She was simply a professional corespondent and had performed the role for Cunningham many times. They were both found dead, each from a single shotgun blast, in his car outside Cobourg. At first the local police took on the case. Then it was discovered that the site was actually a few yards outside the town limits, which made it a matter for the OPP.

I got there before the OPP heavies did, traveling from Toronto with a photographer named Gib Milne in a big chauffeur-driven car, which was a very impressive way to arrive in small town. I knew the Cobourg chief from his days in the OPP, and he showed me the little black book they had found on Cunningham. It was a diary containing the names of prominent Torontonians.

It was clear from the diary that Cunningham also gathered genuine evidence of adultery by people who might not necessarily want divorces, and it seemed reasonable to suppose that the man with the shotgun had been hired to stop his snooping for good. The police had no leads, so my first story from Cobourg was a fairly routine summary of the facts, livened up somewhat by the revelation that Cunningham had died with this diary in his pocket. I did not, of course, mention any names, for fear of libel. But after I'd filed the story, I got a call from the news editor, Jim Kingsbury, who said we were to come up with a full page of stories and photos a day, and he was sending the venerable Roy Greenaway and Fred Davis, another photographer, to help us. They never said anything, but we knew that when Kingsbury or any of the other editors gave such a sweeping order, they were actually passing on a direct command from Harry C. Hindmarsh, our legendary news boss, who'd made the *Star*'s all-out coverage notorious. The little black book angle had obviously tickled him.

Greenaway was one of Canada's best reporters. He had broken many big stories, including the discovery of insulin.

Davis had a reputation for being able to charm his way past anyone. Even people whose aversion to being photographed bordered on the violent became pussycats after a few words from his deep, sympathetic voice. He had done such a good job of charming the Dionne Quintuplets' nurses that he ended up marrying one of them and, at the insistence of the babies' doctor, became the Quints' official photographer.

For the first four or five days, we had little trouble providing the daily page of copy and photos we'd been ordered to get. The reporters in Toronto were helping with stories about Cunningham, who had operated out of a luxury apartment in the Avenue Road hill area. And in Cobourg, the funeral mass for Mrs. Fardella was marred by a skirmish outside the church as her casket was being carried in. Madison Sale, a *Tely* cameraman, took a picture of it and was attacked by one of the slain woman's relatives, a man on crutches, who was suddenly using one of them as a weapon. Sale got a good picture of his attacker and jumped on his motorcycle and sped to Toronto to catch the *Tely*'s early afternoon edition. We got some good stuff from the funeral, as well, and sent it to the *Star* in the chauffeur-driven car.

Also, we didn't find it too hard to locate people who thought they had seen someone standing beside the car on the night of the murders. None of their accounts meant anything to the case, but it gave the newspaper readers a feeling that a major development was near, and they would buy next day's paper to see what had happened. As far as real news went, however, there was very little to report. The OPP had sent in an inspector and a deputy commissioner, but they were not saying much, mainly because they were baffled and had nothing to say.

Greenaway wrote a story about Cobourg's old courthouse and talked to a man who looked remarkably like King Edward VII and claimed to be his bastard son. I did a story about how easily two dangerous criminals had broken out of the town jail a few years earlier, and this, I said, was the place where the Cunningham/Fardella killer would be held if he were caught. But there was no sign of a killer *being* caught, and the story was rapidly petering out. You might think that all we could do then was call the *Star* and say the well had run dry and we were coming home, but it didn't work that way. A command from Harry C. Hindmarsh was exactly that, and you were expected to break your neck obeying it.

So on we went, milking the story for all it was worth. But there came an afternoon when we found ourselves sitting around my hotel room, desperately trying to think of something else to do. We had no new ideas, no fresh angles, and things seemed truly hopeless. But then, out of the blue, Fred Davis said to me, "Go down and get some posies." What he had in mind was a picture of Agnes Fardella's husband, Tony, putting flowers on her grave. All I had to do was buy the flowers and talk the grieving man into posing for us at the cemetery. The stunt had worked for Davis before.

But things were different in this case, and I was quite mindful of the fracas at the funeral as I went up the Fardellas' front steps with a twenty-dollar basket of flowers. Mr. Fardella opened the door, took one look at me and said, "Get the fuck outa here." I stayed where I was, told him that we were anxious to help the police and that a photo of him at his wife's graveside would keep the case alive and increase the chances of someone coming forward with a tip. In situations like that, you do not actually *say* the police have told you a picture would be a help. You just give the impression that it wouldn't hurt the case at all. And it doesn't. In homicide investigations, such photos and stories always spark a flurry of phone calls, and the police know there is always a chance that one of them will provide the solution (look how hard we tried to keep the Allison Parrott murder case alive). But Mr. Fardella wasn't buying my spiel. He flew into a rage, and I am sure that if I had not beat it fast down the stairs, he would have heaved me down them. And that, I knew, would be the fate of anyone else who came to his door talking about pictures, even the sweet-talking Fred Davis.

Back at the hotel, we played poker with some of the cops for a couple days, and the flowers had begun to wilt from all the cigar and cigarette smoke, before it occurred to me that we didn't necessarily need Tony Fardella to place the basket on the grave. As Davis immediately agreed, anyone would do, just as long as we got the picture. I hunted up a character who was usually the beverage room's first customer and offered him twenty dollars to let us photograph him bending over Agnes Fardella's plot with the flowers. We would not, I promised, show his face. He didn't give our proposal a second thought before he accepted.

The picture was sent to the *Star* that night with no information other than that this was a man placing flowers on Mrs. Fardella's grave. The photograph was slotted onto the front page of the next day's first edition, and a night editor with a big imagination wrote the following underline to go with it: MYSTERY MAN AT MURDERED WOMAN'S GRAVE. The edition appeared on the street at about eleven a.m., and not long after that, the OPP commissioner called the deputy and the inspector who had been sent to Cobourg and said the *Star* might have a picture of the killer. "Find out who he is," the commissioner ordered. The two hustled over to our hotel, and we told them about the guy from the beverage room and acted as surprised as they were that the night editor had called him a mystery man and implied that he was connected to the case. The cops laughed. Both were veteran police investigators and knew that reporters sometimes had to make the news.

And go on making it. Greenaway and I were told that if the police weren't getting anywhere on the case, we should do our own investigating, which is easier said than done. We were unable to find out anything the police didn't already know and soon found ourselves facing a newsless weekend, with nothing for the Monday morning paper.

It was Gib Milne who saved our bacon. He struck up a conversation with a woman in the lobby of the hotel. When he mentioned that he was in Cobourg covering the murders, she seemed troubled and claimed to have been a friend of Cunningham's. She disappeared for a while, then came back, showing signs of having drunk quite a bit in the meantime. Drunk or not, she appeared to be genuinely grief-stricken, and we were exuberant at the thought that we had lucked onto a fresh angle and had actually turned up an important witness.

Her story, which she told hesitantly and in obvious fright, was that she'd had an appointment to meet Cunningham in Cobourg late on the night of the murders. As she was driving there, she had seen his car parked on the shoulder of Highway 2, where the murders had subsequently taken place. A well-dressed woman was standing beside the car, so rather than risk embarrassing Cunningham by stopping, our informant had driven on by and waited at their rendezvous. When he didn't show, she had left.

This, we knew, was a version of the case that the police had not heard. Although she said she didn't want her name published for fear the killer would get her, the woman had no objections to a picture. Gib got a shot of her sitting up on my dresser with a good bit of leg showing, and I wrote a straight story about a mystery woman who claimed to have seen a woman near the car shortly before the murders. The story implied that what this new witness said could be important to the investigation, which was an obvious conclusion.

The same night editor who had handled the mystery man at the cemetery decided that my story needed to be "firmed up." So he wrote a quotation, which he attributed to a police officer, saying the mystery woman's story threw new light on the case.

The story and photo were a one-day wonder. They got big play and increased street sales, and everyone at the *Star* was happy. In Cobourg, though, the OPP investigators were not at all amused by our second mystery person, whom they tracked down the next day. She had sobered up and had no memory of ever talking to us. They charged her with public mischief and said we could expect to be called as witnesses. The charge, however, was dropped soon after we left Cobourg. We had been there for two long weeks. In the hundreds of murder cases I have had something to do with over the years, I've usually had some little inkling, some suspicion, of who the murderer was or might have been. In that Cobourg case, I didn't have a clue. Neither did the police, and the mystery is now almost half a century old.

Back in Toronto, the war was, of course, the continuing big story. But crime still sold lots of papers. That was my beat and, at work, I saw few reminders of the war, except on the odd occasion that I visited the chief's office. Draper, the vicious anti-Communist, had a huge map of the Russian front on his wall, and he could talk endlessly about the brave Russian soldier and the gallant Russian people. The map was studded with different colored pins, and every day he changed their positions according to the battle reports in the newspapers. When the Red Army finally defeated the Germans at Stalingrad, he seemed in awe of their victory. He never said "Germans," though. He always called them "*Huns*," giving the word a ring and an emphasis that left no doubt of a hatred for them that went back to his service in the trenches during the First World War.

But as I have said, Draper did not have much to do with day-to-day policing or police reporting, and my central memory of him from the war years is of the one time he did get involved and helped kill a story that, in normal times, I would've paid money to be allowed to write. It had to do with a Peeping Tom who was frightening women all over the east end by spying on them as they were undressing for bed. One day, all the crime reporters were summoned to the office of Mayor Fred Conboy. Draper was there when we arrived, and the mayor, speaking as chairman of the Toronto Police Commission, told us that the peeper had been caught by the diligent work of a police officer. The culprit, Conboy reluctantly added, was a police inspector. But not just any inspector. It was Cherry Nose, the man who, a decade before, when he was a sergeant, had thrown me out of that house in the west end!

What had happened was that a patrol sergeant had noticed that, on nights when the peeper was reported, Cherry Nose was frequently walking his dog in the same area, often far from his home. Like most policemen, the sergeant hated Cherry Nose. He began keeping an eye out for him and, one night, saw the inspector lead the dog into an alley. The sergeant followed and found Cherry Nose masturbating as he peered through an apartment house window. The sergeant crept right up to him, tapped him on the shoulder and said, "Good evening, Inspector. You're under arrest."

What a story! As Charlie Oliver had said, it was indeed a long alley that didn't have any ash cans, and I could hardly wait to get to my typewriter. But, as the mayor then said, he didn't have to remind us that policemen were not exempt from the draft and the force was seriously understaffed. Not only could this story severely damage the morale of the men who had not left to join the armed services, it would also hamper the drive to recruit temporary replacements. In short, he was asking us to make a wartime sacrifice and kill the story. We bought it and, with handshakes all round, promised not to write a word. In fact, we didn't even tell our editors. Cherry Nose was never charged. He resigned and took his pension, and the public never learned that a police inspector who'd been quoted as saying he'd beefed up his squads to catch the peeper was himself the owner of what one woman had described as the "ugly face looking in the window."

That was my last brush with what you might call official censorship, though another incident from around that time illustrates how you often had to make judgment calls and decide when it was prudent to play ball with the cops. This one had to do with a string of armed drugstore holdups. The police decided that every evening till the robber was caught they would have a man staked out in the back of every pharmacy in the downtown area — which was a fairly simple thing to arrange in those days, because policemen were not paid overtime. Soon after the stakeouts began, the robber held up Webb's Drug Store on Yonge Street, near Wellesley. The clerk was the owner's wife, who had been told to signal the cop as soon as the robber showed. But she didn't give the alarm until the guy was on his way out the door. The cop rushed from his hiding place and fired his pistol. The bullet bounced all over the shop, hitting bottles in the dispensary and ricocheting off the ceiling and the walls and the floor and finally lodged in the woman's rear end. She was not badly injured, but even so, a cop accidentally shooting a citizen in the bum is front-page news. But before we could write anything, John Chisholm, the chief of detectives, collared us and said, "Look, can we make some kind of deal here?" His point was that the bandit was probably still unaware of the stakeouts and likely to strike again soon. So we sat on the story and, sure enough, a couple of days later, the robber tried to hold up another pharmacy and was nabbed by the policeman waiting in the back.

13

The Triple Hanging

I OPENED THIS BOOK WITH A MEMORY of the cold night in 1945 when I covered the execution of three men in Fort Frances. That was the largest number of people to die for a single murder in Canada since the late 1920s, when four men were hanged in Montreal.

Actually, four men were responsible for the horrendous death of Mrs. Viola Jamieson in a remote shack out along the railway line that ran through Fort Frances. They were William Schmidt, Eino Tillonen and two brothers, George and Anthony Skrypnyk. Mrs. Jamieson's daughter, Bernice Casnig, had told Schmidt that her mother, who sold bootleg liquor to loggers, had a hoard of money stashed away. Schmidt and the Skrypnyks went there one night when the woman was out and ransacked the place. They found $1,200. Bernice was not impressed. Her mother, she said, had at least $20,000. Schmidt and the Skrypnyks returned to the shack, taking Tillonen with them. This time Mrs. Jamieson was there, and they tried to make her tell them where she had hidden the money. They burned her with torches made of newspaper and, when that didn't work, laid her out across the kitchen stove. The poor woman had only $700, hidden in a jar under a rock, but her torturers got only the $40 she had on hand, and Mrs. Jamieson died of her burns about ten days later.

The OPP Criminal Investigation Branch assigned Chief Inspector Albert Ward and Inspector Frank Kelly to the case and it automatically became a job for me, because the OPP CIB was part of my beat. I covered the case from Toronto until the spring of 1944, when I went up to Fort Frances for the trial of the four men. I had just returned from the police games in Detroit, a big annual event in those days, and when I got off the train at Union Station, I simply boarded another one for the trip west. Also aboard were Dr. Smirle Lawson, the chief coroner of Ontario, and Dr. W. L. Robinson, the pathologist who had gone up to do the postmortem on Mrs. Jamieson. Already in Fort Frances were Cecil L. Snyder, the deputy attorney general, who would be prosecuting the case, and Mr. Justice Fred Barlow, who, until recently, had been Master in Chambers at Osgoode Hall and was about to hear his first murder trial.

My understanding was that the attorney general, Leslie Blackwell, had been outraged by the terrible crime and ordered an all-out effort to catch and convict the guys responsible. Nevertheless, on the train there was considerable speculation that the defense would try to get the murder charge dropped by arguing that the men had not intended to kill Mrs. Jamieson and that she would not have died had she received prompt medical attention. But that never became an issue. Kelly and Ward had put together an airtight case, complete with confessions that left no doubt that Schmidt had planned the crime and suggested the fire torture. Perhaps, with experienced lawyers, those men would not have been convicted of murder (they certainly wouldn't have been today, because *intent* to murder has to be proven), but their defense was no match for Cecil L. Snyder. The trial lasted hardly a week, and at the end of it, Mr. Justice Fred Barlow ordered each man, in turn, to stand while he read the death sentence to him, concluding each time with the chilling words "and may God have mercy on your soul." When I spoke to Barlow in the hotel lobby a few hours later, he was still emotionally shaken by what he had done and was clearly in need of a stiff drink.

The four men were to hang on December 6. But Tillonen's sentence was commuted to life in prison, in exchange for the help he had given the police, and Schmidt got a stay of execution by claiming that others had been involved and the real instigators had not been caught. That was quickly proven to be false, and he filed an appeal with the Supreme Court of Canada. George and Anthony Skrypnyk had no money for an appeal, and the townspeople began to fear that only they would hang, while Schmidt, the ringleader, escaped the noose. The townspeople engaged Joe Sedgwick, a Toronto lawyer, to seek a stay of execution for the brothers until the Schmidt appeal was heard. It was granted. Schmidt lost his appeal and the executions were set for one minute past midnight on the morning of March 1, 1945. I was sent back to Fort Frances with Fred Davis, the photographer.

We found that the townspeople had also been upset by how the executions were to be done. The jail was right across the road from a residential area. The jail was also small and, unlike jails in larger centers, had no permanent scaffold. For a previous hanging, they had built a scaffold in the jail's yard, and the condemned man had been visible from the street, standing on the platform before the trap was sprung. The locals did not want that to happen again, so when we arrived, the hangman, a carpenter from Toronto, was busy building an improvised scaffold inside the jail. This required cutting a hole in the floor of the nurse's dispensary, which was on the second floor, next to the room where the governor's children slept. The noose was to be attached to heavy ceiling beams. Below the nurse's room was the prisoner reception area, and the hangman also had to cut a hole in the floor of it, down to the basement, in order to ensure a sufficient drop. Some months earlier, in anticipation of the frozen winter ground, three graves had been dug beside the town's lawn-bowling green. There was a wooden fence around the site, with signs warning children not to climb over.

The hangman told me his name was Smith, which may have been true. That's about all I got out of him, except the impression that he was an ordinary working stiff. Traditionally hangmen were named Ellis because we couldn't use their real names and so called them by the name of a famous hangman in England, and you never got too close to them, because whenever they were on a job, an OPP officer was always around to keep people like me away. It was generally believed that the hangman was paid a retainer by the attorney general's office, plus a fee and expenses for each execution. At that time, the fee was $400. Many years later, it was discovered that Ontario had kept a hangman on retainer long after capital punishment was abolished in Canada.

The day before the execution, we learned that the portable steel trap, which was to go over the hole in the dispensary floor, was due to arrive by rail from Toronto. When Fred and I got to the station, hoping to get a picture of it being taken off the train, we were told that the hangman had already been there and had been greatly distressed to learn that his parcel had been mistakenly shipped to Sudbury. He was, we assumed, now back at the jail, hastily building a wooden trap.

That afternoon, Davis and I visited the home of Schmidt's parents. They were sitting at the dining room table, alternately reading passages from a large Bible and praying, either for a stay of execution or their son's soul. "I cut the wood the trap door is made from," Mr. Schmidt said.

He worked, he said, at a local lumber yard, and earlier that day, a stranger had come in and said he needed various pieces of wood of certain lengths in a hurry. Mr. Schmidt had cut the wood to the specified measurements, unaware that he was serving his son's executioner.

At other executions I'd covered, there had always been a crowd of curiosity seekers and people who were opposed to capital punishment outside the prison. In Fort Frances that night, the street was absolutely deserted. Of course, it was late and terribly cold, but it was still strange. The only people to be seen were the odd passerby, who would stop and stare for a moment at the lit jail; the occasional cop, who would come out and walk once around the building; and Fred Davis, me and Bernice Casnig. I had called and asked her to come down to the jail for a photograph at midnight. During the trial, she had shown no remorse at her part in her mother's death, and now she seemed utterly unconcerned that a former boyfriend was about to die. Fred posed her on the veranda of a house across the street, asking her to hike up her skirt and show a little more knee. He was after a "cheesecake" shot of the kind editors loved in those days. Bernice complied. Fred's flashbulb exploded like a gunshot in the quiet night. The cops came pouring out of the jail with their pistols drawn, heading straight for Fred. "Don't shoot!" he screamed, and dropped his camera.

The disgusted cops went back inside. Shortly afterward, the Skrypnyk brothers were hanged together, back-to-back, dropping from the nurse's room down through the reception area to the basement, where a doctor was stationed to pronounce them dead. Schmidt died alone.

When it was done, the police and jail guards came out with three plain wooden coffins and took them to the graves. The pile of earth beside each grave had been heated in advance so it would be soft enough to be shoveled back into the hole after the coffin had been lowered and pails of quick lime dumped on top of it.

14

How My Hustle for a Scoop Almost Landed Me in Jail

IN 1946, **JOHN CHISHOLM FINALLY REPLACED** Dennis Draper as chief of police, and I succeeded Athol Gow as the *Star*'s senior crime reporter. That was also the year of the sensational Evelyn Dick murder trial, during which I came very close to being thrown in jail and fired.

Draper's removal was engineered by the mayor, Bob Saunders, an astute criminal lawyer who knew how to get along with newsmen and the police. He was aghast at the force's poor public image and low morale. Hatred of Draper now ran so deep that at annual police association meetings at the Carls-Rite Hotel, with the chief sitting right there at the head table, certain cops and reporters hid behind the pillars and yelled "Chisholm for Chief! Chisholm for Chief!" Saunders had heard them and knew that "Chisholm for Chief" had become a watchword throughout the police department. As a lawyer who'd successfully defended five murder suspects, he also knew the inside operations of the police force and the excellent work John Chisholm was doing. As far as he was concerned, no more outsiders were to be brought in as chief. But Draper was not a member of the police pension fund and had no intention of living on his small army pension. Saunders got around that by arranging for the police commission to retain Draper in an advisory capacity at $2,000 a year. Of course, no one expected him to advise anybody on anything, and he was never again seen at police headquarters after his departure on January 17, 1946.

The Evelyn Dick story broke quietly on March 16, 1946, with a brief statement from the Hamilton police that a man's torso had been found that day by a group of boys hiking in the Mountain area of the city. The condition of the body, and the bullet wounds discovered by the pathologist, pointed to a gangland killing. The police went ahead on that assumption and were checking out their list of missing men, when a detective remembered a woman named Evelyn Dick coming in earlier that month and asking if her husband, John, had been arrested. The detective had asked her what he might have done to get himself arrested, and she'd said stealing streetcar tickets from the Hamilton Street Railway, where he was a motorman. The woman had left the police station without filing a formal missing person report.

John Dick had in fact vanished, and his bosses at the street railway were concerned. A steady employee, he had bought a supply of tickets on March 6, but had not turned up to drive his Sherman Avenue route. Dick's aunt, with whom he had been living, and who also regarded him as a pretty steady fellow, was worried, too. She filed a missing person report. Three days after the discovery of the torso, the police identified it as the remains of her nephew, John, a mild-mannered man of the Mennonite faith.

He had, the police learned, married Evelyn the previous October and left her on Christmas Eve, eleven weeks later. After the wedding, Dick had discovered that his bride was not the childless widow she had claimed to be. She had a retarded three-year-old daughter, who was living with her parents, Alexandra and Donald MacLean. The child, she said, was from a marriage in Cleveland to a soldier who had been killed in action overseas. That was not the only surprise in store for Dick. He and Evelyn were living in a house they had bought on Carrick Avenue. But as he eventually discovered, mainly by hiding in the bushes outside the place, his wife was also renting an apartment, where she entertained friends and her lover, one William Bohozuk, a husky member of a rowing club. When Dick left Evelyn, her mother and daughter came to live with her on Carrick Avenue. Dick told his buddies at the car barns that he had been played for a sucker. He had made the down payment on the house, but only Evelyn's name was on the papers.

I learned hardly any of this during the few days I spent in Hamilton immediately after Dick's torso was found. That came out much later, and about all I really knew at the time was that Inspector Charlie Wood of the OPP had been sent out from Toronto, and that he and Sergeant Clarence Preston, a Hamilton detective, were in charge of the investigation and reporting directly to Cecil L. Snyder, the deputy attorney general. But they were saying absolutely nothing. The other papers were getting nothing, either. So I returned to Toronto, having uncovered little more than some lurid rumors about Evelyn Dick, who was well known in Hamilton as what was then called a party girl. That did not mean she was a prostitute, but she did like a good time and cruised the better hotels, looking for action. It was said she kept a record of the prominent businessmen she had partied with in a little notebook.

Even though I was back in Toronto it was still my story, and I was instructed to stay on top of it, but the police continued to say nothing and I had plenty of other work to do. Then, a few days after my return, I ran into Art Keay, a Toronto detective and former Olympic runner, who was also just back from Hamilton, where he had gone to pick up a car thief. Knowing I had been there, as well, and thinking I knew more than I did, he said, "That was quite the thing down in Hamilton, eh?"

I said nothing to betray my ignorance and he proceeded to tell me how he had been waiting at the Hamilton police station for his thief to be released, when a group of detectives came in. "Look what *we* found," one of them said, and showed him a club bag in which there was a dead baby. Apart from a portion of the face, the child had been completely encased in concrete. The cops had raided Evelyn Dick's home and found it in an upstairs bedroom closet. Also in the bag were many thousands of dollars' worth of street-car tickets. The infant had been strangled with a cord that was still around its neck.

As Keay told me his story, my heart sank. I was sure the competition would have all the details in their early editions. About all I could do now, I thought, was write a good follow-up and take my lumps for missing the original break. My first call was to Cecil L. Snyder, whom I had gotten to know during the Hot Stove trial in Fort Frances. When I asked him to confirm the baby in the concrete, he must have assumed I knew a lot more about it, because he also mentioned several other details, including the fact that human teeth and bone, presumably the remains of John Dick's head, legs and arms, had been found among furnace ashes that had been used to fill a mud hole in Evelyn's driveway.

TORSO CASE BABY FOUND DEAD was the headline over my story in the *Star*. As it turned out, no other paper had any of the information I had uncovered. Simply by being in the right place at the right time, I had come up with a clean scoop. The story even took prominence over the trial of Fred Rose, the Labor Progressive MP who had, the previous year, been unmasked as a Soviet spy by Igor Gouzenko. From what Snyder had told me, I was also able to predict that the police were about to make an arrest. This proved to be more than accurate. Evelyn Dick, William Bohozuk and Donald and Alexandra MacLean were all charged with the murder of John Dick. Evelyn and Bohozuk were also charged with the murder of the baby. At the preliminary hearing, the Crown dropped the charge against Alexandra MacLean, who became a witness against her daughter. Her most damaging testimony related how she had taken Evelyn's daughter down to Sherman Avenue so she could wave to John Dick as he went by in his streetcar. They didn't see him, and when Mrs. MacLean later mentioned that John had not been on his run and asked if anything was wrong, Evelyn had replied, "He won't bother me anymore. He's dead and now you shut your mouth."

No one ever confessed to anything in this case, so a couple of basic mysteries remain. The first is, why was the baby killed and left in the closet? The other is, why did Evelyn ever marry John Dick in the first place, and why was he killed? It's quite likely that the baby, who was born sometime before Evelyn married John, was an unwanted love child. After it was strangled, Evelyn probably intended to throw the concrete-weighted bag into Hamilton Harbour, but never got around to it and took the grisly package with her when she went to live with her husband, presumably still intending to get rid of it someday.

As for John Dick, it's important to know that Donald MacLean, Evelyn's father, also worked for the Hamilton Street Railway, and he had a key that fit all the fare boxes on the streetcars. At the time, the streetcars were crowded every day, but the company was losing money. Donald MacLean, on the other hand, had something like a quarter of a million dollars in the bank, infinitely more than anything he could've saved from his salary. So it seems reasonable to assume that he was robbing the fare boxes and also stealing streetcar tickets, which could be sold at a discount at the steel mills and elsewhere. From what Charlie Wood told me later, and from what I gathered intuitively at the trial, I suspect John Dick caught on to what Donald MacLean was doing and then one of two things happened. Donald prevailed upon Evelyn to come on to Dick and thus neutralize any threat his knowledge might pose. Or maybe Dick was already in love with Evelyn and threatened to blow the whistle on her dad if she didn't marry him. In any case, they did marry, and the supposition was that Dick again became a threat when he discovered his wife was seeing Bohozuk and had no plans to stop. Apart from her odd visit to the police station earlier in the month, the cops had no reason to think twice about Evelyn until the detectives told her that the torso found on the Mountain was indeed the remains of her husband. They had given similar news to many widows but had never elicited a reaction like the one they got from Mrs. Dick. She just said, "Well, don't look at *me*. I didn't do it." That got them thinking and looking, and not long afterward they charged her with vagrancy, the catchall charge used in those days when the police wanted to hold someone for extensive questioning about a crime for which there was not yet enough evidence to lay a specific charge. The amazing answers that Mrs. Dick gave to the questions Wood and Preston asked her left no doubt in their minds that she was one of her husband's killers, and formed the basis of the prosecution's case against her.

She, Donald MacLean and Bohozuk were each to be tried separately for the murder of John Dick, with her trial being the first. It began in Hamilton shortly after Labor Day, with Mr. Justice Fred Barlow, another acquaintance from Fort Frances, on the bench. In the preceding months, the preliminary hearing had aroused considerable interest because it was held behind closed doors. The rumor of choice, particularly in the *Star* newsroom, was that the press and the public had been barred from the hearing in order to protect the prominent men who'd partied with Mrs. Dick. But that wasn't it at all. The real reason was that the prosecution had argued that the statements Evelyn had given to Wood and Preston should remain an absolute secret until they were read to a jury, and the court had agreed.

I was assigned to cover the trial with two other reporters, Marjorie Earl and Alf Tate, and Frank Teskey, a reporter-photographer. Alf and I were to do the running copy of the testimony, while Miss Earl did color stories. The prosecutor was Timothy Rigney, a veteran Crown attorney from Kingston, who was quite accessible to the press. A few days into the trial, I got wind of the secret statements and asked him about them. He freely admitted their existence and said he would be introducing them in a few days. Of special interest, he added, would be Mrs. Dick's responses to questions related to the bloodstains found in a car she had borrowed around the time of her husband's murder. I asked him to let me see copies of the statements in advance, assuring him that they would not be used until they had been read to the jury. He refused.

But, as old Charlie Oliver had said, if you can't get it from one source, go to another. So I hunted up Mrs. Dick's counsel, John Sullivan, and asked him if he knew about the statements. He said they were in the transcript of the preliminary hearing. Moreover, each night after adjournment, the transcript was left in the barristers' room at the courthouse, which was never locked.

That night, I went to the barristers' room, expecting to find a transcript of perhaps a couple of thousand words. There were actually three separate statements and they each ran to many thousands of words, far too much to copy by hand. Today you could put even a document of that size through a photocopier in minutes, but we had no such things then. So I tucked the transcript under my arm and went back to the hotel to get Marjorie Earl, who was a speed typist. She and I went down to the telegraph office, where she sat at a typewriter and copied Wood's and Preston's questions and Mrs. Dick's answers as I read them to her. It was fantastic stuff, and at one point, I remember, I had to stop and exclaim that if this was admitted as evidence, Evelyn Dick was a dead duck.

Her statements were partly contradictory and all of such extravagant absurdity that even the most inexperienced police officer would have realized she was covering up a murder. She began one statement, for instance, by declaring that she had learned her husband was seeing other women from two odd visitors who had come to her house. The first was a woman who was looking for John and who quickly left when Evelyn told her she was his wife. Then a man who looked like an Italian came to the door and said, "John is breaking up my home and we're going to fix him."

Later, in response to questions about bloodstains in the borrowed car, Evelyn said she had got a phone call from someone who'd told her, "This is one of the gang from Windsor. We caught up with your husband and put him out of business because he was warned to lay off the wife of a friend. She's going to have a baby now and he paid us to have John killed."

This man, she said, had also told her to get a car and meet him on the Mountain, which she had done and stopped near a "beautiful car parked in the dark." She said a man had got out of the car, dragging a bag behind him, and when she asked what it was, he said it was part of John and he had been paid to put him out of business. The man, Mrs. Dick said, had tossed the bag into her car and instructed her to drive him to another part of the Mountain, where he had taken the torso out of the bag, dumped it and then had her drive him to a downtown hotel.

By this time, as the transcript clearly showed, Wood and Preston were utterly flabbergasted by what they were hearing. "Why would this man call you up the Mountain to get you to drive the body in your car, when he was already almost there in his own car?" Wood asked.

His car couldn't stay, Mrs. Dick replied, because the other men in it had to do a job in Toronto and some alcohol-running in Windsor.

"How did you feel when the man said part of John was in the sack?" Wood asked. She said she didn't know how she felt, which prompted him to ask if she was glad John had been done away with. "Well, no," she said, "but it was a pretty mean trick to break up a home. He had so many enemies."

It was dawn before Miss Earl and I had finished. Because of the length of the statements, and since they were of no immediate use, I sent them to the *Star* by bus express, to be set in type on a hold-for-release basis. Political speeches, financial reports and news releases are handled this way by newspapers every day, and I warned the office that Mrs. Dick's statements could be used only when they had been ruled admissible by the judge and read to the jury, which was likely to happen soon.

John Sullivan argued against admission of the statements on the grounds that Evelyn had made them while being held on the vagrancy charge, which he maintained gave the police no right to question her about a murder. But the Crown's argument prevailed, and during a morning session a few days after I'd sent the copy to Toronto, Justice Barlow ruled that the statements could be read. Timothy Rigney told me that he and Harvey McCulloch, another Crown attorney, would be ready to read them into the record, question and answer, when the jury returned from the afternoon recess.

That put me in a quandary. If I waited till after the recess to signal the *Star*, there would be no time to insert the statements into the last two editions of the day. Also, it was Saturday. There were no papers on Sunday, and Monday was Thanksgiving, when we didn't publish, either. Therefore, if we did not run the statements that day, the *Globe and Mail*, which did publish on Thanksgiving Day, would scoop us on Monday morning. But, I figured, since the statements were now as good as read to the jury, and we already had them in type, there would be no harm in getting a jump on the court. I rushed to a nearby teletype and flashed the go-ahead to the paper.

No one could have foreseen what happened next.

At the *Star*, Stan Davies, the afternoon news editor, was actually yanking display advertisements to make room for the eight full columns of fascinating conversation between Evelyn Dick, Inspector Wood and Sergeant Preston. Back in Hamilton, the fifteen-minute recess was stretching into half an hour. Then there were whispers that one of the jury members had died. No one could say what had happened, but eventually a sheriff's officer came by and said a doctor had been called to attend to an ill juryman, though the fellow might still be able to sit for the reading of the statements.

I called the *Star* to see if there was any chance to yank the statements and was told that one edition was on its way out the door with a screaming headline that read MOBSTERS SLEW HIM — MRS. DICK and a subhead saying JOHN KILLED FOR BREAKING HOME HIS WIFE SAYS. The last edition was already on the press, all set to go, and we had no way of stopping it at that stage.

All I could do then was wait. And wait. Finally, word came that the doctor had said the juryman was better, but not well enough to continue and it would be best to let him rest over the weekend in the hotel where the jury was sequestered.

I know one thing. That juryman wasn't as sick as I was. I didn't need a lawyer to tell me that it would be impossible to exaggerate how seriously in contempt of court I had placed myself and the paper. However, after returning to Toronto for the weekend, I did call the *Star*'s lawyer and explained what had happened. I was, I added, on speaking terms with the judge, and perhaps I could go to him before the court opened on Thanksgiving Day, which was not a holiday as far as the trial was concerned, and humbly admit the error and tell him how it had occurred. I think the lawyer was right when he told me to stay away. The judge could have accused the paper of interfering with justice.

At the opening of the session on Monday morning, before the jury came in, a lawyer for the Hamilton *Spectator* helpfully drew Justice Barlow's attention to last Saturday's *Star* and the MOBSTERS SLEW HIM headline. "I am aware of it," the judge replied curtly, his jowls shaking. As I later learned, he had become aware of it that Saturday night at the Ontario Club, which was then in downtown Toronto and the unofficial headquarters of the Ontario Liberal party. Barlow had not *seen* Mrs. Dick's statements, and his first clue to their contents came when a fellow club member started talking to him about them in astonishing detail.

The *Spec*'s lawyer, speaking as an officer of the court, as all lawyers are, moved a motion of contempt against the *Star*. Barlow ordered a copy of the paper filed as an exhibit and said, "I will deal with the matter at the conclusion of the trial."

The *Star* was prepared to argue that because the statements had been ruled admissible, it and I were not in contempt. I didn't place much faith in that, especially after I had lunch with the court reporter who traveled with Justice Barlow. He told me that the judge was extremely angry and it looked like a $5,000 fine for the paper and two months in jail for the man responsible for obtaining the statements. He was shocked when I told him I was to blame. He said the judge figured a member of the *Star*'s staff had got the transcript from someone in the attorney general's office at Queen's Park.

With the prospect of going to jail and being fired before or afterward looming over me, I decided to go against the lawyer's advice and confess to Justice Barlow. He didn't want to believe me, thought I was covering up for someone else, and I had to convince him that I had taken the transcript and copied the statements. When he asked how I knew the statements were in the transcript, I said I couldn't tell him because it would get an innocent man in trouble. He seemed to appreciate that, and I explained how, if the paper was fined for contempt, I could expect to lose my job and my career as a reporter would be over. "It's a very serious thing" were his parting words as I left his chambers. I agreed, and went back to reporting the trial.

The jury returned a verdict of guilty with a recommendation of mercy. When Mr. Justice Barlow asked if she had anything to say before he passed sentence, Mrs. Dick's dark eyes flashed up toward him and she said, "I would like my case appealed." Barlow sentenced her to death. The courtroom was absolutely silent, except for a leaking steam radiator, which had hissed throughout the trial. After Mrs. Dick had been taken away, Barlow heard the Crown's submission on the contempt motion and said he would consider it in his chambers in Toronto and give a judgment later. That night, Evelyn Dick's mother told reporters, "I love her dearly. She has been such a lovely child." And, sometime later, Mrs. Mac-Lean gave her daughter a Christmas present in the form of money to appeal her sentence.

John J. Robinette, who later became the dean of Canada's criminal lawyers, was retained. He argued that Mrs. Dick had not been sufficiently warned before her statements were taken and drew attention to the delaying tactics used by a police officer when a lawyer had tried to get into the room at the police station where she was being questioned. Above all, he stressed that she had been questioned about the murder while being held on a vagrancy charge, the legality of which was a burning issue in legal circles at the time. The five-member appeal court panel unanimously agreed that Evelyn should have a new trial and ruled that her statements were inadmissible.

I wasn't assigned to cover her second trial. For one thing, even though my scoop on the statements had sold two extra truckloads of the *Star* in Hamilton that weekend, the paper was reluctant to push my luck with Evelyn Dick any further. Also, Athol Gow had retired that fall, and I really had enough on my plate as his replacement.

The second trial centered on the testimony of a young man who claimed to have seen the torso in a car he had been engaged to pull out of some mud with a team of horses. The woman he had seen in the car, he said, was Mrs. Dick, and one of the men was William Bohozuk. He had not gone to the police about this and had not been heard from during the first trial. He had told a friend, who had passed the story on to the police. To counter his evidence, Robinette produced the police chief of Dundas, a town near Hamilton, who said the witness was a notorious liar. With the kid's credibility gone, and without the self-incriminating statements Evelyn had given to Wood and Preston, the prosecution's case collapsed and the jury found her not guilty.

She still had to stand trial for murdering the baby, who had been registered as Peter David White to match the name of her fictitious husband. At the trial, Evelyn said he'd been a naval lieutenant and went from there up to an admiral, but always added that he was killed in action. The key point was that the child left the hospital with its mother in a taxi and was not seen again until the detectives opened the bag they found in the closet.

A verdict of manslaughter was returned and Evelyn Dick was sentenced to life in prison. She served eleven years in the women's penitentiary at Kingston before being secretly released in late 1958. After that, she completely disappeared, despite a considerable effort by various members of the media, including me, to find her.

Donald MacLean was convicted as an accessory after the fact in the murder of John Dick — the only person to be punished for the torso slaying. He did about four years of a five-year sentence and died in 1955 at age seventy-six, his huge bank savings long gone on legal fees. William Bohozuk faced two trials, for the murder of the baby and of John Dick. In each instance he was defended by G. Arthur Martin, who also became one of Canada's best criminal lawyers and is now a retired appeal court justice. "You couldn't hang a dog or even whip one on this evidence," Martin contemptuously told the court at one point. Bohozuk was acquitted on both counts.

As for Mr. Justice Fred Barlow's judgment on the contempt motion, I spent a good part of late 1946 and early 1947 wondering if I was going to hang before Evelyn Dick did. The reporters at Osgoode Hall told me they periodically looked into the matter and were always told it was pending. And it kept on pending. Barlow never did deliver the judgment. Now and then, I would see him on Bay Street and nervously recognize him with a slight bow, but we never spoke. He would just give me a wink and continue on his way to lunch at the Ontario Club.

15

Getting Away with Murder

NOVELISTS AND TV SCRIPT WRITERS often come up with plots that suggest there is no such thing as a perfect murder. Two intriguing cases I covered in 1947 say they are wrong.

The first involved the murder of a pretty twenty-two-year-old woman named Christina Kettlewell, who was killed while honeymooning with her new husband, Jack, at a cottage on the banks of the Severn River. The *Star* jumped on the story after it was revealed that Ronald Barrie, Jack Kettlewell's inseparable friend, the best man at the wedding and owner of the cottage, had gone on the honeymoon, too. He had been present when the cottage unaccountably burst into flames, shortly after Jack and Christina had sustained mysterious head wounds.

Barrie, a former ballroom dancer who dabbled in real estate and sold insurance, told police that he had left the bride and groom sitting in the living room of the cottage and taken his morning stroll. On his return, he'd found Jack Kettlewell in the kitchen, dazed from a head wound, which he blamed on Christina. Next, Barrie said, he had dragged Jack outside on a mattress, and, minutes later, a fire broke out in the kitchen area. After looking around for Christina and not seeing her anywhere, he had rushed Kettlewell to the Orillia hospital. Then, he said, he had come back to the burned cottage and subsequently found Christina dead in the river at a picturesque place called Dinnertime Rapids. A pathologist later said she had drowned after sustaining a head wound, which was caused by a blow, not a fall.

Now, if you are to make some sense of what is to follow, it's important to understand that Christina was murdered not long after the appeal court threw out Evelyn Dick's murder conviction, and the police were discouraged and confused about how to legally question homicide suspects. As various officers expressed the dilemma to me, "How do we find out what went on if we can't ask the people anything?" In short, the police were feeling somewhat hampered by the Dick decision, which perhaps explains why Barrie and Kettlewell were not questioned more vigorously about what had gone on at the cottage.

Proceeding with the new ruling in mind, Inspector Tom Wright of the OPP CIB and Sergeant Dave Adair of the Gravenhurst office asked Barrie to assist them in the investigation. He proved most cooperative and used his skills as a trained typist to compose a three-thousand-word statement for them in the office of the Orillia police chief. I saw him doing it. Fred McClement, a *Star* photographer, and I arrived in Orillia late on a very rainy night. We were not allowed into the police station, but we could see Barrie through the window, his fingers flying on the typewriter keys. The police never showed us the statement, but I gathered that it contained no more than what I have outlined above.

Anyway, that night the police let Barrie go, and Art Cole of the *Globe* and I took him to a café. On the way, he said he would tell us everything, but he proved to be maddeningly evasive when we finally sat him down. He didn't know how the fire had started. He didn't know how Christina had got to Dinnertime Rapids. He was, he said, completely mystified. As the investigation proceeded over the following month, he continued to promise "explosive revelations" to reporters, but always said he couldn't reveal them right away, because the police didn't want him to let them out. The police said he was free to say whatever he wished.

The first hint I got that the inquest would hear some remarkable evidence came in late June, when I interviewed the coroner a few days before the inquiry was to convene in the courthouse at Bracebridge. The coroner told me they had suicide notes in Christina's handwriting, which Barrie had given them, and he had also produced a note that indicated she had planned to kill Kettlewell and herself "because he doesn't give a hoot for me and I can't live thinking he is married to someone else." But these notes, Barrie had explained, were not what they seemed to be. Christina had written them at his suggestion, in order to get Jack to marry her. She had done that, Barrie said, and Barrie had kept them.

Investigation by police and reporters also revealed that Christina's family, who lived in Mimico, a small town just west of Toronto, had known nothing about her plans to marry Jack Kettlewell. Her sisters had not approved of her friendship with him because of his excessive devotion to Barrie. As one sister told reporters, wherever Christina and Jack went, Barrie tagged along. "They were never alone," she said. The wedding had been small and quiet, with none of the bride's family in attendance; and, as was revealed at the inquest, the ring that Jack Kettlewell slipped onto Christina's finger had been borrowed by Barrie from a female friend "as a symbol."

Clare Hope, a veteran of many murder prosecutions, was assigned to be the Crown counsel at the inquest. He seemed determined that the jury should bring in a verdict of homicide, with the finger pointed directly at Barrie.

For example, under Hope's questioning, Kettlewell told of a couple of occasions when he and Christina had become quite ill after eating meals prepared by Barrie, but they had recovered with only minor stomach cramps. And Hope was relentless in his questioning of Kettlewell about his relationship with Barrie, which had begun when they were schoolboys. Finally, after being reminded he was under oath and that the matter could be further investigated, Kettlewell admitted he and Barrie were lovers.

More bizarre evidence unfolded when Barrie took the stand and was asked about a receipt signed by Christina, which indicated that she had repaid a debt to him of $15,000. In conjunction with this, the jury heard a statement that Barrie had given the OPP three weeks after his typewritten one. In it, Barrie said Christina had approached him in April about a loan of $2,000. He said he had given it to her without asking why she needed it. Then, he said, she had asked for $4,000 more and told him she was being blackmailed by four or five young men who had "criminally attacked" her at a church social and were threatening to tell people what had happened if she didn't pay them. In all, Barrie said, he had, without telling Kettlewell, given her a total of $15,000 before saying he could not lend her any more. She had then, the statement continued, said she would have to get it from another friend, but did not mention who this might be. Then, Barrie said, Christina had suddenly turned up with bundles of money and repaid the whole loan. She said friends had loaned her the cash.

Rapists in those days still faced a sentence of life in prison, and this tale of blackmail in reverse clearly tried the Crown counsel's patience. "Do you mean to tell this inquest," Hope demanded, "that men who raped a woman would then blackmail her?" Barrie said it was true.

Hope's questioning was the strongest I had ever heard at an inquest, particularly when he accused Barrie of being Kettlewell's lover. Barrie denied it. Hope persisted, saying, "Aren't you what is known as a cocksucker?" Barrie replied by stamping his foot and saying, "I resent that, Mr. Hope. I am not." This while the courtroom was crowded with high school students who had taken the day off to hear the inquest.

The police also testified that they had turned up double-indemnity insurance policies on the Kettlewell couple's lives, with Barrie the beneficiary in each case. To me, it looked like a diabolical murder plot, laid well in advance, but Hope, who was an extremely able cross-examiner, could not pin Barrie down. In his final remarks, he described the whole affair as "a heterogeneous conglomeration of attempted murder, homosexuality, poison and an unbelievably mendacious story told by Barrie — a tangled skein of deception, of love, real love and bestiality." However, the jury returned with a verdict that Christina had died at the hands of a person or persons unknown. The police were left to sort it out. They couldn't and the case went down as one of the province's most mysterious deaths.

As I have noted earlier, such mysteries always sold papers, and our readers didn't have to wait long for another one. The Kettlewell inquest had hardly ended, when Tommy Lytle, the city editor, called and told me to hop the next train through Bracebridge and get up to Cochrane and join Frank Teskey, who was already there, covering the rape-murder of a Toronto nurse who had been working at the Lady Minto Hospital.

Valair Vandebelt, an attractive girl of the same age as Christina Kettlewell, had been strangled and raped at the back of a cottage property on Silver Queen Lake, a few miles outside Cochrane. She had gone there with some other nurses and two young men for a Saturday night beer party. When it came time for her and the other nurses to leave, so they could beat the strictly enforced curfew at their residence, Valair was quite drunk and refused to go. No coaxing could make her change her mind. So, while the other nurses rushed off to the residence, the two young men, Rocco Sisco and Roger Gauthier, stayed with Valair, trying, they said, to get her sober enough to sneak into the residence later on.

Valair's body was found at the site the following day. The police, of course, immediately questioned Sisco and Gauthier. But again the appeal court decision in the Dick case got in the way, and the young men told the police little more than the same story they gave to Teskey and me: they had eventually given up trying to get Valair to go back to the residence and had gone home themselves, leaving her there.

Inspector Wilford Franks of the OPP murder squad came up from Toronto and, with the local police, put together a circumstantial case. The Crown attorney ordered Sisco and Gauthier charged with murder. After all, they were the last to be seen with the nurse, and circumstantial evidence had often resulted in murder convictions and hangings. The police believed that the pair had been too eager to stay behind

The moment I made up my mind to be a newspaperman in 1930. I'm on the upper row at the left. Nat Turofsky is second from the left in the first row, and Jessie MacTaggart, one of the few women reporters of the era, is in the front row, second from the right.

The Toronto Police Athletic Association Field Day in 1935, at which Red Ryan was guest of honor. LEFT TO RIGHT: Duke McGarry, a track and field official; Chief Coroner Dr. Malcolm M. Crawford; Judge Frank Denton; Eddie Murphy, a criminal lawyer; Red Ryan; and City of Toronto Controller Percy Quinn.

SUMMONS TO A PERSON CHARGED WITH AN OFFENCE.

CANADA, PROVINCE OF ONTARIO,
COUNTY OF YORK,
CITY OF TORONTO.
TO WIT:

TO ...Gwyn Thomas...................................

109 Merrick Street

....
of the said city.

WHEREAS you have this day been charged before the undersigned, a justice of the peace in and for the said city of Toronto, for that you, on the 28th day of March in the year 193 7, being the Lord's day, at the city of Toronto, in the county of York, being a merchant, tradesman, artificer, mechanic, workman or labourer, unlawfully did sell or publicly shew forth or expose or offer for sale, or purchase goods, chattels or other personal property, the same not being conveying travellers or His Majesty's mail by land or by water, selling drugs or medicines, or other works of necessity or works of charity, contrary to an Act to prevent the profanation of the Lord's day in Upper Canada, (being chapter 104 of the Consolidated Statutes for Upper Canada, 1859, section one) in such case made and provided.

THESE ARE THEREFORE TO COMMAND YOU, in His Majesty's name, to appear before me on Fri day, the 9th day of April next, at two o'clock (Toronto time) in the afternoon at the City Hall, in the said city, or before such other justice for the said city as shall then be there, to answer to the said charge, and to be further dealt with according to law.

Given under my hand this 31st day of March in the year 193 7, at Toronto aforesaid.

A justice of the peace for the city of Toronto.

NOT TO BE SETTLED OUT OF COURT

The summons I was served in 1937 for buying tobacco on Sunday. I was fined $2.00, but the judge recogized me as a reporter who covered his court, and waived the $1.50 court costs. The $2.00 was a good chunk out of my $18.00 a week salary.

I'm at extreme left in this photo, in which a group of reporters and editors gathered around reporter Tommy Lee when a CP telegraph boy arrived with a singing birthday telegram.

Bob Hope at Camp Borden, there to entertain the troops in 1944. LEFT TO RIGHT: Frank Teskey, *Star* photographer; Jack Karr, entertainment editor; Hope; and Athol Gow, the *Star*'s senior crime reporter at that time.

As the night police reporter, 1936.

My wife, Marjorie, and my son, Ron, posing with the highways story, for which I won a National Newspaper Award in 1954.

In Tijuana with Stephinino Dinino and 14-year-old prostitute Sabina. Dinino was charged with tossing his bride over a cliff while on their honeymoon.

I was president of the Press Club in 1949. Seen here at that year's Byline Ball are Ontario premier Leslie Frost (CENTER) and Bob Farquharson, managing editor of the *Globe and Mail* (LEFT).

Gordon Sinclair (CENTER) with Beland Honderich, former publisher and now chairman of Torstar, owner of the *Toronto Star*. The occasion was a TV show on Gord's 80th birthday.

With Mrs. Ruth Hindmarsh and John Duncan, when John and I were
honored in 1979 for 50 years' service at the *Star*. I stayed on for 10 more years.

My son, Ron, with Staff Supt. Adolphus Payne at a party judges and lawyers threw
for Payne Feb. 7, 1974, on his retirement. Ron is now a judge.

Picture taken March 3, 1989, the day I retired.

Igor Gouzenko (LEFT) and Mrs. Gouzenko, leaving the courthouse building in Toronto on June 6, 1975. This picture by *Star* photographer Bob Olsen is the only news photograph ever taken of Gouzenko.

Portrait taken by *Star* photgrapher Fred Ross.

when Valair said she wasn't leaving, and that they had killed her when she resisted their sexual advances. It was a plausible assumption, and most of the people I spoke with in Cochrane agreed with it.

John J. Robinette, who had won the appeal for Evelyn Dick and then got her acquitted at her second trial, was hired by the families of the two Cochrane youths. At the preliminary hearing, Robinette's cross-examination of the other nurses revealed that Sisco and Gauthier had showed a genuine desire to get Valair back to the hospital. There was, he argued, simply too much doubt to send the young men to trial for murder. The magistrate agreed and freed them.

The police and the Crown attorney talked about further proceedings by direct indictment, but nothing ever came of it. Several years later, the case took a strange twist when a new suspect emerged, although it was too late for any action to be taken or even to gather the evidence needed because the man had died. This was a local businessman. He had a cottage near the one where the beer party was held and had been there that night. According to the story the police later heard, he saw Sisco and Gauthier leave and came on to the intoxicated nurse, chasing her to the back of the property, where he strangled her with a plastic belt from her dress. This version seemed as plausible as the circumstantial case against Sisco and Gauthier. The lesson a reporter learns from such developments is never to be sure that anyone is guilty, no matter how strong the suspicion.

But, as the end result of yet another 1947 murder shows, even when the evidence points right at someone and he is duly punished, you can't help wondering if justice was really served. The murderer in this case was clearly a young man named Austin Craft, a prisoner at Kingston Penitentiary. He was a simpleminded soul with the look and smile of Stan Laurel of the Laurel and Hardy comedy team, and one of the prison guards, John Kennedy, had taken a liking to him. Every day, Kennedy drove into town to get the prison mail and he frequently allowed Craft to ride with him from the prison garage to the gate. Another prisoner, Howard Urquhart, got someone in Toronto to come to Kingston and slip a revolver wrapped in cloth into one of the car's hubcaps while Kennedy was in the post office. Shortly before Kennedy's next run, Urquhart gave the pistol to Craft and hid in the trunk of the car. As usual, Craft sat beside the driver. At the gate, he shot the guard to death, took over the wheel and raced away, stopping soon afterward to let Urquhart out of the trunk.

The police caught them almost immediately. They were each charged with murder and tried separately the following year. I covered both trials. Craft turned down pauper's counsel and conducted his own defense, with advice from a lawyer provided by the court. He was found guilty and sentenced to hang.

Urquhart, the instigator of the crime, enjoyed the services of Norman Borins, a clever defense lawyer, who had for many years been a top Crown prosecutor. This was Urquhart's second murder trial in about two years, the first one arising out of the killing of a storekeeper on Mount Pleasant Road in Toronto. Only their youth had saved Urquhart and three other young men from the gallows. This time, his lawyer saved him with an eloquent address to the jury in which he argued that Urquhart had wanted Craft to use the gun only to get the guard out of the car and facilitate the escape, not to kill him. On the morning the case went to the jury, I walked from the hotel to the courthouse with Urquhart's father, an employee of the Toronto Transit Commission. I felt quite sorry for this man, who, for the second time in two years, was attending a trial where his son's life was at stake. Suddenly, he bent down and picked up a new penny that was lying on the sidewalk. "This means good luck. He'll be found not guilty," Mr. Urquhart said. A few hours later, the jury came back with a manslaughter verdict, and the prisoner's grinning father held his lucky penny up for me to see.

Austin Craft was left to face the noose alone, and I was hardly fifty feet away when it happened. A few days before his execution, I got a tip from the OPP inspector who'd worked on the case that Craft had written a sermon and given it to a minister, to be read the night he was put to death. A murderer delivering a sermon from the grave! That was real *Star* stuff, so I rushed to Kingston and tried to track down the sermon. I called a lot of ministers, who hadn't heard anything about it, so I went to the Frontenac County Jail, because the governor would have had to have forwarded any letter from a condemned man. It was about ten o'clock on a Sunday evening. Craft was to die soon after midnight. I didn't know what I was getting into.

I had a bottle with me and ended up having a fairly convivial time with the governor and the sheriff who was in charge of the hanging. The conversation, as I recall, had a lot to do with a game the Canadiens had played the previous evening. As midnight neared, they got ready to go up to the room where the scaffold was, and one of them said to me, "Give us five minutes and come up those stairs." In other words, he was saying I could watch the execution. I knew, of course, that I would not be able to write anything about it. The attorney general of the day, Leslie Blackwell, was all in favor of hanging but didn't like newspaper stories on the subject, so anything I wrote would have got these men in trouble.

The rounds of drinks in the office probably had something to do with it. Anyway, when I got about halfway up the iron stairs, I lost my footing and slid down, the bottle making a tremendous racket as it hit the steps. For some reason, it didn't break. But the noise had alerted the hangman, the same guy who had done the Fort Frances triple hanging, who was waiting for me when I got to the top. He grabbed me and said he wanted me to stand between him and Craft. "I never look into the face of the man I have to hang," he explained.

So, moments later, when two guards brought Craft out of his cell for the walk to the scaffold at the other end of the corridor, he saw me, not the hangman. He gave me a faint, nervous smile, an indication that he recognized me from his trial. The hangman slipped behind him, dropped a hood over his head and cinched his arms tightly, high up behind his back, with a wide leather belt. This last procedure was done to tighten the neck muscles, which made it easier for the noose to break the neck, thus minimizing chances that the prisoner would die of slow strangulation.

Craft was led down the corridor to the scaffold, accompanied by a minister, who was reciting the Lord's Prayer in a high-pitched, almost inaudible voice. I saw the noose put around Craft's neck and that was it for me. I tried to get back down the stairs before the trap was sprung. I didn't and was all but paralyzed by the crash that echoed through the silent limestone jailhouse. Still on the stairs, I had a swig from my bottle, and suddenly the hangman was there. "I'll have one," he said, and took the bottle. There was very little liquor left when he handed it back.

I had actually met this fellow one other time, in December 1946, while covering the hanging in Welland of George and Elizabeth Popovich for the murder of a bootlegger. Today the Popoviches would have been convicted only of manslaughter, if that. But it was a different age then. Mrs. Popovich was the first woman to hang in Ontario since 1936, when Elizabeth Telford, who had fed arsenic to one too many husbands, was executed in the Woodstock jail.

No one was allowed near the Welland jail, but I learned that the police and officials had booked a hotel beverage room for a party, which was to begin shortly after Mr. and Mrs. Popovich were hanged at midnight. I slipped in and saw the hangman, who was wearing a tuxedo under his winter coat, standing by himself. I moseyed over and asked him how the couple had met their fate. He told me they had said to say good-bye to everybody and thanked the police for being so kind to them. I didn't believe that at all, but before I could ask anything else, a big OPP sergeant grabbed me by the coat collar and threw me out of the room. The drinking went on till one a.m., when the group moved to the nearby Half Moon Restaurant. I followed and saw that the hangman was sitting by himself. Not even the cops and prison people wanted anything to do with him. I did, though, and quietly took the booth behind his. Before we could resume our conversation, however, the OPP sergeant spotted me and threw me out of the restaurant.

I didn't get much out the hangman after the Craft execution, either. The next morning, though, I did find the minister who had read the dead man's sermon to his congregation.

He wouldn't release it without permission from the sheriff. The sheriff would not give it, so I called the attorney general and within a few minutes had the okay to print the sermon. It was really just a couple of rambling pages scribbled in a school notebook, urging young people to obey their parents and lead a life free of crime. Hardly worth the trip to Kingston.

16

The Long, Slow Death of Stanley Buckowski

I **SAW HIM DIE, WRITHING IN AGONY** for thirteen minutes, his body in convulsions, his mouth hidden by froth, as the deadly cyanide did its work in the gas chamber at San Quentin Penitentiary, near San Francisco. The viewing area outside the Green Monster, as the gas chamber was known to Death Row inmates, was crowded on that sunny May morning in 1952, but probably only two of the people there, Ron Poulton of the *Tely* and me, really knew who the dying man was and what he had done. Most of the others were a committee of ministers from the Southwest Ecumenical Council. They had been charged with recommending the most humane way of carrying out capital punishment and were on a tour of U.S. prisons, observing methods of execution.

The dying man was Stanley Buckowski of Toronto, a former member of the Royal Canadian Air Force, who had got to know the power of handguns when he was fifteen years old. That first gun was only a toy, but he'd pointed it at a motorist parked in High Park and stolen his car. The police caught him in the car and sent him home with an order for his father to thrash him. It did no good, and Buckowski went on to rob service stations and clothing stores. When he joined the

RCAF, he was posted to Saskatchewan, where he stole drugs from the base dispensary to feed the addiction he had developed. Posted back to Toronto, he married. While his wife, Jean, worked as a waitress to pay the bills, Buckowski was burglarizing houses to get money for drugs. Acting on a tip, the police searched his home and found a pile of burglary loot. He was sent to Burwash, the rough prison farm near Sudbury, for eighteen months.

The time in jail cured Buckowski's drug addiction, but when he was released he turned to liquor, which he needed to bolster his courage for armed robberies. On July 30, 1949, he went to a locker in the Central YMCA, got one of his guns and had a few belts from a bottle. He then proceeded to the busy Loblaws on Parliament Street, where he went into the manager's office and told the man to open the safe and get down on the floor. One look at the gun and Buckowski's twisted, pockmarked face told the manager that to otherwise might cost him his life. Buckowski stuffed handfuls of money into his pockets and ran for the door. The manager shouted, "Stop that man!" One of the clerks tried and got shot in the leg.

Out on the street, a number of passersby gave chase. Among them was Arthur Layng, a young RCAF vet, who was out with his wife and daughter. Layng grabbed the robber. Buckowski shot him in the leg. Layng did not let go, so Buckowski shoved the pistol into his stomach and fired. Layng died there on the pavement. This did not deter the other pursuers, who were so close to Buckowski that he couldn't get to his car, which was parked on a nearby side street. He dashed madly through back alleys, yards, laneways and even through two houses, before he shook off the posse. At a hotel on Sherbourne Street, a few blocks west of the supermarket, he called a taxi and went back to his apartment.

I was in Detroit at the time, attending the police games, a pleasant annual junket that was one of the few perks of my job. I remember Chief John Chisholm being summoned to a telephone to take a call from his acting chief, who informed him that a citizen had been murdered on Parliament Street. There was, of course, no way I could have known that almost a year and a half later, I would be in California and the murderer would be handing me the biggest scoop of my career.

When we returned to Toronto, Sergeant Adolphus Payne and other detectives had begun the tedious task of searching the route of Buckowski's flight. Payne gave untold hours to the job, many of them literally on his hands and knees, continuing the search long after his colleagues had given up finding anything. In fact, a couple of days later, I can recall hearing someone at headquarters asking at one point, "Where's Dolph?" and someone else replying, "He's still back there crawling around, the crazy bugger."

But Payne's doggedness paid off. On one street, where the killer had run in the front door of a house and out the back, Payne looked under rear stoops of almost every house on the block before finding a gray double-breasted pinstripe suit jacket. There was no tailor's label, but the pockets contained a pair of gloves and two .38-caliber revolver bullets. Payne kept on looking, and eventually came upon a woman who remembered that the dog next door had been spooked by something at about the time of the chase. Payne took a look and, under the back steps in that yard, found a pair of gold-rimmed eyeglasses, which, along with the jacket, turned out to be the crucial links between Stanley Buckowski and the murder of Arthur Layng.

Establishing the links took weeks of foot slogging by detectives, who had to canvas every made-to-measure tailor shop in Toronto, carrying samples of cloth cut from the discarded jacket. Payne was confident that the tailor who had made the garment could be tracked down. A mannequin wearing the jacket was put in the window of a store near the spot where Layng had been killed. That brought no results, but finally a tailor in the east end recognized the stitching on the jacket as his late father's work. Detectives went through the store's sales records and found that the pinstripe suit had been made for one Stanley Buckowski three years earlier. In the meantime, other detectives had been canvassing the city's opticians, and this paid off, too, with the discovery that the glasses Payne had found had been prescribed for, and bought by, Mrs. Jean Buckowski.

By then Buckowski was in New Orleans, staging holdups and burglarizing houses. Jean joined him there. In January 1950, they moved to Los Angeles. They lived in a hotel for a while and then found an apartment. Buckowski was back on heroin. One night while he and Jean were out for a stroll, he spotted a darkened house. He went up and rang the doorbell. Getting no answer, he cut the telephone line and broke in through the back door. The seventy-eight-year-old widow who lived alone in the house heard the noise and got out of bed just in time to bump into Buckowski in the darkness. She screamed. He shot her to death and fled.

Like most criminals, Buckowski felt he would never be caught, and went on burglarizing homes and offices in search of cash to buy heroin. At one place, the police found a broken rope hanging from a skylight and rightly figured that the burglar would be injured. A search of emergency wards revealed that a man who'd signed in as Frank T. Miller had been treated on the night of the break-in for a fractured ankle, given a walking cast and released. Buckowski's ankle still hadn't healed when the L.A. police got a tip and caught up with him while he was buying heroin on Skid Road.

The police lodged Buckowski on the ninth floor of a hospital. He escaped out a window, climbing most of the way down a rope made of bed sheets, then dropping the final thirty feet without injury. There was no sign of him for more than two months. Then a Los Angeles patrolman with a good memory for faces spotted a man in a car on Sunset Boulevard who looked very much like a man whose photo was on a wanted poster back at the precinct house. As the cop strolled toward the car, Buckowski got out ran into a park, where he was soon surrounded in a clump of bushes. He answered the police calls to surrender with a fusillade of shots, and the gunfight continued until Buckowski ran out of ammunition for the five pistols he had with him.

That was in May 1950. Buckowski was booked under the name of Miller. His fingerprints were routinely sent by the Los Angeles police to FBI headquarters in Washington. Much earlier, the RCMP had also sent Buckowski's prints there, but for whatever reason, a considerable amount of time passed before the man in L.A. was properly identified. Of course, as soon as the Toronto police found out where Buckowski was, they wanted him for Layng's murder. And they *would* have got him, because all the California authorities had on him was a burglary, the drug bust, the escape and a shoot-out in which no one had been hurt. But at this point another element of the story came into play.

The Toronto police knew that immediately after he killed Layng, Buckowski had gone up to Wasaga Beach, on Georgian Bay. A Toronto couple named Gloria and Robert McKay had been there at the same time. They were later found dead of gunshot wounds in widely separate parts of Toronto. In yet a third location, the police had found their abandoned car and pulled a palm print from it. The police were eager to talk to Buckowski about the McKay murders too, and asked the L.A. cops to palm-print him. They did so and, while they were at it, compared the result with outstanding palm prints of their own. You can imagine how pleased they were to find that it matched a print found in the home of an old lady who had been shot to death. The California authorities decided to keep Buckowski for themselves. He was tried and quickly sentenced to die in the gas chamber. The Toronto cops, however, still wanted him face the courts here.

Now, I didn't learn most of this until the fall of 1951, after Buckowski had been sentenced. One of the advantages of hanging around a place like police headquarters for two decades is that you get a feel for when things aren't quite what they seem. In this case, Adolphus Payne seemed unusually busy. I knew he had the Layng murder, but that was stalled and there was nothing else that I knew about on his plate. So I asked him what was up. Unlike some other cops, who would lie to you, if Payne didn't want to talk about something, he would just say, "I can't tell you anything about it, so don't ask me." Which was what he said then. But I asked around and soon found out that the police had connected Buckowski to the McKay killings and were trying to get into San Quentin to question him. That was a scoop in itself, and I thought of a dandy way to break it.

I wrote a memo to the city editor, explaining what I had learned and suggesting that I go to San Quentin to try to interview Buckowski. Even if he wouldn't see me, I said, I still had enough information for a great scoop, and a San Quentin dateline would make it even juicer. I sent the memo off, but heard nothing about it. Borden Spears, the city editor, was away on vacation, and his replacement, probably thinking that I was just angling for a nice out-of-town trip, as reporters will do, had put my memo on the spike. However, Spears found it when he got back, and sent it into Harry C. Hindmarsh with a note saying, "This sounds like the best crime story of the year. I suggest we send Mr. Thomas." It came back to Spears with the words "Send him right away."

Today you *can* go places right away. But this was 1951 and getting seats on airliners was not that easy. A while later, Spears saw I was still around and said, "Get out of here! I've told Mr. Hindmarsh you're on your way." I explained about the flight. "Get out of here. You're supposed to be gone." The memo had been on the spike for at least ten days, and all of a sudden it was "*get outa here.*" Not unusual at the *Star*. I did the travel arrangements at home. Frank Teskey was to have gone with me, but his wife, Helen, chose that moment to give birth to the tenth of the twelve children they were to eventually have. Doug Cronk, another photographer, was assigned to the job, instead. We took a bus to Buffalo, then flew to Dallas and from there to San Francisco. It's odd, thinking about that flight today. Three years later, Doug was killed in an airplane, along with Alf Tate, with whom I'd worked on the Evelyn Dick trial and many other stories. Alf had spent months trying to get permission to fly with a photographer into the eye of a hurricane on a U.S. Air Force weather plane. Permission finally came, and they, the plane and the crew disappeared over the Bermuda Triangle.

The rule at San Quentin was that if you wanted to see a prisoner on Death Row, you filled out a request form in the warden's office and it was taken to the condemned man. If he wished to see you, fine. If he didn't, too bad. I later learned that a couple of police inspectors from Toronto had already been there and Buckowski had refused to see them. If I'd known that beforehand, I probably wouldn't have written the memo. Surprisingly, he agreed to see me.

I was taken to an interview room, and Buckowski was brought in by a large, husky guard, who sat well out of the range of our voices. The killer was a pitiful sight, suffering from a dreadful rash on his face. It was for this reason, I think, that he refused even to consider allowing his photograph to be taken. We were lucky enough to be in there at all, but the *Star* wanted a picture of me interviewing him. No amount of coaxing, including a promise to take the picture at a distance so the rash wouldn't show, could make him change his mind. However, he did agree that Doug could sit in the room while we talked.

But when the burly photographer came into the room, Buckowski took one look at him and said, "You're a *cop*. You guys aren't going to pull that one on me." Mindful of the fact that if he chose to leave it would be all over, Doug and I produced our police press identification cards and did everything we could think of to calm the man down and make him believe we were who we said we were. It worked, and Buckowski withdrew his claim that he had seen Cronk with other detectives when he was taken into Toronto police headquarters some years earlier.

Even so, I really believe the interview would've still gone badly, except I suddenly remembered that Buckowski had attended Essex Street Public School, which was in the neighborhood where I grew up. I'd not gone there, but a lot of my chums had, and they had all talked glowingly of a Miss Washington. So I said, "Stan, you went to Essex Street Public School, didn't you? Did you know Miss Washington?"

His face lit up and his eyes filled with tears. "Did you know her?" he asked. "Oh, she was wonderful to me. Do you take shorthand?" The question took me by surprise, and I had to say I didn't. "Then you'd better write fast," he said, "because I talk fast and I'm not gonna stop."

And by God, he did talk fast and hardly stopped for a moment. He began by telling us details of the Layng killing and went on from there to Wasaga Beach and his reason for killing the McKay couple, which has to go down as one of the most bizarre explanations of a murder ever. It all hinged upon the fact that the use of artists' sketches of crime suspects was still something new in law enforcement. After Layng was killed, a *Globe* cartoonist named Jack Booth had come to the scene and, with the help of a Toronto police identification officer, spoken to the many witnesses and produced a sketch of the killer. The witnesses must have been exceptionally observant and Booth very good, for when Buckowski saw the sketch on the front page of the *Globe* up in Wasaga the next day, it was such a startling likeness he thought it was a police file picture of himself. He had, remember, tossed away his wife's glasses, which he needed for reading. The caption under the sketch explaining that this was just an artist's conception of the killer was lost on him.

He panicked. Thinking it was too risky to drive his own car back to Toronto, he hitched a short lift from somebody who dropped him near where the McKays were parked on the side of the road, resting before tackling the heavy holiday traffic returning to town. When Buckowski yanked open a rear door and got in the back seat, his gun already drawn, he found they were asleep, with Gloria's head on Robert's shoulder.

"I put the gun to his neck and told him not to try any funny stuff," Buckowski told me, the tone of his voice suggesting that he wanted us to believe Robert McKay was responsible for what happened. When they got to Toronto, Buckowski went on, "He got mad and started to run the red lights anywhere there was one and that's why I shot him. She screamed and I shot her, too, and brought the car to a stop."

The McKays were murdered at Eglinton Avenue West and Oriole Parkway. Buckowski drove north to Armour Heights, near where the 401 now crosses Avenue Road. He intended to dump both bodies there. But after he'd dragged Robert out of the car, a dog started barking in a nearby construction site, so he drove down to the Christie Street Hospital parking lot, a location he knew because he had been treated there when he was in the RCAF. Before leaving the lot, he dumped Gloria into the trunk and, because he didn't have the heart to kill it, left the McKays' pet spaniel tied to the bumper. The next day, worried about his fingerprints, he came back and wiped the interior of the car down, somehow missing the vital palm print.

The McKay murders had been the subject of numerous theories and speculation. The guesswork ended as far as the public was concerned when the *Star* published Buckowski's Death Row confession. I was later told by the circulation manager that my scoop occasioned one of the very few days when the complete press run had been sold. Hindmarsh, who was by then president of the *Toronto Star*, ordered double headlines and, to make sure the public knew the story would be in the Saturday paper, directed that summaries of it be sent by taxi to all the radio stations in time for their noon newscasts. When I returned from San Francisco, he made it a point to come from his office and shake my hand, chuckling between drags on his ever-present cigar and gloating over the frenzy the *Tely* must be in, trying to catch up with us. Several months later, the Buckowski confession earned me the first of the three National Newspaper Awards I was to receive during my career.

The big scoop was in October 1951. Buckowski was gassed in May 1952. Neither I nor the *Star* had any wish for me to go down and see him die. Hindmarsh had been assigned to see more than a few executions in his own time as a reporter and had no desire to hand out similar assignments. However, the paper got a tip that the *Tely* had heard we were planning nothing big for the Buckowski execution and had sent Ron Poulton to San Francisco, their idea being to beat us with an on-the-spot story and other features on the day the killer died. The city editor called me at home and said to get down there as fast as I could.

I did. From my hotel, I called Hartley Teets, the new warden of San Quentin, who told me a man from what he called the Toronto *Telegraph* had been there the day before, trying to get Buckowski's permission for an interview. But, Teets said, Buckowski wasn't seeing anyone, not even his own attorney, nor would he sign a document that would automatically put off the date of execution. I asked who the attorney was. The warden told me, adding that his office was just around the corner from where I was staying.

I went there, and the attorney told me Buckowski was determined to die and had brought a halt to the appeal process, which might have prolonged his life for years. The last time he had seen his attorney, he had just shouted at him to stay away. There were twenty-one other prisoners on Death Row, among them Caryl Chessman, the condemned rapist and best-selling author, who by then had kept himself out of the gas chamber for eight years. Buckowski had told his attorney that Chessman seemed bound to die in the end anyway, even though he was only in there for rape. He, he said, was down for murder, so what chance did he have?

After leaving the attorney, whom Poulton had not visited, I called the *Star* with a story that began, "With twenty-four hours to live, Stanley Buckowski refuses to see anybody and says he wants to die as soon as possible." It was on the front page the next day, and again we beat the *Tely*. You see, they had a big story all ready to go on the day of the execution and were happily sitting on it, thinking the *Star* wasn't anywhere near San Francisco.

The execution was, as I have said, sickening. Ron and I and many of the touring ministers couldn't watch the whole thing and turned our faces to the wall. But when it was done, Ron and I had to write it up fast and get our stories to Toronto in time for the big afternoon editions. The Americans were always coming up with last-minute stays of execution, so there was no way our papers could assume Buckowski had died on schedule. They had to hear it from us.

Either to save money, or because they thought it was faster, the *Tely* had arranged for Poulton to call his story to Vancouver, whence it would be relayed to Toronto. The system somehow broke down in Vancouver and they missed their deadline, which was how I ended up scooping the *Tely* twice in two days. I did it by going to the nearest phone booth and calling the *Star* direct. My description of the execution was sent to the presses with background copy that had been written in advance, and my story also contained a nice bit of color about the ministers who were touring around, observing executions. I never did learn what their consensus was, but the ones I spoke to after Stanley Buckowski was pronounced dead said they were most impressed with the death by firing squad they'd seen in Utah.

17

The Boyd Gang Saga

ON THE EVENING OF NOVEMBER 5, 1951, I got a call at home from the night city editor, who told me to get over to the Don Jail because the police radio was broadcasting descriptions of three men who had escaped.

I arrived to find several reporters already outside the jail, but no news was released until the provincial inspector of prisons came out for a press scrum on the steps about ninety minutes later. The three escapees, he told us, were Edwin Alonzo Boyd, a bank robber; William (Willie the Clown) Jackson, a mugger; and Lennie Jackson, another bank robber, who had been arrested after a holdup in Bradford, north of Toronto. Before being captured, he had shot at his OPP pursuers with a machine gun. Lennie, who was no relation to Willie Jackson, walked with the aid of an artificial left foot. Someone had recently sent him a new foot, in which had been hidden a number of hacksaw blades. Somehow, the jail's fluoroscope had not detected the blades, and Boyd and the two Jacksons had used them to saw through a barred window, via which they escaped down a rope made of bed sheets.

The only one of the three names to ring a bell was Edwin Alonzo Boyd. A month before, I had called him a master bank robber in a story about how he'd staged a successful string of one-man robberies and had then been caught after using a partner for the first time. The son of a retired policeman, Boyd had served as a commando during the Second World War. He returned to Toronto with an English war bride and got a job as a streetcar driver. Maybe money was short. Maybe he missed his wartime adventures. Whatever the case, he began robbing banks, stuffing his nostrils and cheeks to alter his Errol Flynn-like appearance. He always hit suburban banks, because the police out there had large areas to patrol and could not respond to alarms as quickly as city cops could. Which does not mean robbing suburban banks was an entirely safe thing to do. In those days, all bank managers and tellers had guns in their offices and cash drawers and were expected to use them if they got a chance. To keep their employees sharp, the banks had a pistol range in the basement of the old Bank of Toronto building downtown, and bank staff from all over the city were sent there for target practice. This went on until the late fifties, when the all-but-inevitable accident happened. In a bank at Dundas and McCaul, a manager fired at a robber, missed, and another employee was killed by the ricocheting bullet.

Boyd later told Adolphus Payne that he was chased and shot at several times and more than once heard bullets whistling past his head. There is no record of him ever firing his own gun. By himself, he robbed seven banks and then, for some reason, teamed up with a man named Howard Ferguson Gault. He also decided to rob a Toronto bank, picking one at Lawrence Avenue and Yonge Street. While Boyd held a pistol on the staff, Gault collected $12,000 from the cash drawers. Gault was captured during the getaway. Not knowing this, Boyd went back looking for him and ended up in a north Toronto police station, where he met, for the first time, the man who was to play a leading role in the remainder of his life.

This was Detective Sergeant Adolphus Payne, who was determined to get Boyd to admit responsibility for the seven other holdups. He told him it would be better if he owned up to what he had done, although if the truth be told, Boyd had disguised his face well and Payne knew it might be impossible for witnesses to identify him. Boyd insisted he knew nothing about the seven holdups. Payne told him he didn't want to get rough, but he would if Boyd didn't tell the truth. At this point, Boyd later said, Payne gave him a crack on the jaw. Whatever he did, it worked. Boyd gave Payne a complete confession. The next day, after being remanded in court, he was taken to the Don Jail and put in a cell with Lennie Jackson and Willie the Clown, whom he had never seen before.

After the escape, the trio hooked up with Boyd's brother, Norman, and one Steve Suchan, who was a friend of Lennie's, and embarked on a spree of a dozen or more bank robberies that went on for almost four months and thrilled and terrified the town and sold a lot of newspapers. The gang's standard method was for Boyd to jump onto a counter and cover the bank staff and customers with a Sten gun, while the others grabbed the cash. They were getting what was, for the time, big money: $25,000 to $47,000 a score, taken mainly from branches where extra funds were on hand to cash payroll checks, which indicated the gang was doing its homework.

After the first robbery, witnesses' descriptions of two of the bandits fit Lennie Jackson and Alonzo Boyd. I referred to the robbers as the Boyd Gang in my story, thus becoming the first reporter to use what soon became one of the most notorious names in Canadian crime. In all of the many stories I wrote about these criminals, I always called them the Boyd Gang and referred to "the master bank robber" as their leader. However, later on, Payne and other cops told me that the real leader of the outfit was Lennie Jackson. If anything, Boyd was something of a sucker, standing up there on the counters, an easy target for anyone who cared to take a shot at him.

Willie Jackson left the gang early. He was a loser, and the police had predicted that he would be the first of the escapees to be arrested, which was what happened after an informer heard him bragging about the escape in a Montreal bar. Between jobs, Boyd didn't associate with the others, perhaps out of caution, and possibly because he just didn't care for liquor. Steve Suchan and Lennie Jackson did, and they hung out at a west-end tavern where it did not go unnoticed that, whenever the papers were headlining the latest sensational bank robbery, they always had rolls of money to pay for the drinks.

Now, I'm not exactly sure how the next part of the story began to emerge, but I am certain that Sergeant of Detectives Edmund Tong had one or more informers in that tavern. Tong was a friend and a man I admired as a resourceful and fearless policeman. Sometime in February 1952, I went home with him one evening and was astonished by the man I saw there. With rounders on the street, he was a tough, swashbuckling detective with no respect at all for criminals. At home, he was a gentle and loving father and husband. His daughter, I remember, showed me a scrapbook in which she kept clippings of the newspaper stories he was mentioned in.

Toward the end of February, with Marjorie and Ron away at the time, I invited Tong and his partner, Sergeant Roy Perry, to my house for a steak dinner. Before we ate, while Perry and I had a beer in the living room, Tong shut himself in the kitchen and talked in whispers on the phone for well over half an hour. It must have been a fascinating conversation, because he forgot about the cigar he'd put aside and it left a long burn on our kitchen table. I asked Perry who he could be talking to. Roy said he didn't know. He was probably talking to an informer, and Eddie never revealed the identity of his finks to anyone. Even so, when Tong finally came out of the kitchen, I asked him who he'd been on the phone with. He said, "Never mind," and apologized profusely for the burn on the table. He and Perry hurried through their meal and went back on the road.

A few days later, on March 6, 1952, I was working at the *Star* office, keeping one ear on the police radio, when I suddenly heard Perry screaming, "Ed's been hit. Get an ambulance!" He himself was shot moments later as two members of the Boyd Gang fired bullet after bullet into their police car, trying to kill them.

What had happened, I am certain, is that during his long

telephone conversation in my kitchen, Tong had learned something about the gang's next job. I suspect it had to do with the type of car that would be used. Anyway, on March 6, Tong and Perry stopped a certain car near College and Lansdowne. They were not expecting trouble. If they had been, both officers would have got out of the police car with their guns drawn. But Perry, who had left his gun locked in his desk at lunchtime, remained in the car, while Tong approached the other vehicle, his gun still in its holster.

The two men in the other car were Steve Suchan and Lennie Jackson. Tong didn't know Suchan, who wasn't really an underworld face, having mainly worked as a fraud artist. Tong did know Jackson, and knew he was a potential killer, but on that day, Lennie was heavily disguised. When Tong was a couple of steps away from Suchan's side of the car, the shots were fired and he crumpled to the ground. The bandits then shot out the windshield of the police car, trying to kill Perry, and they nearly did it.

Tong lay in hospital for seventeen days before he died. At first, the word around headquarters was "Eddie's tough, Eddie's strong, Eddie'll survive," and for a while I believed that. Then, a week after the shooting, I was talking on the phone with Inspector John Nimmo, who had been Tong's partner for years. "Do you want to see Eddie?" he asked. I said I did, and he said, "Okay, I'll take you in." Tong was lying there motionless. The bullets had gone through his lungs, and his spinal cord had been severed. I bent down and whispered in his ear, "Eddie, it's Jocko." He responded with a slight movement of one finger, which surprised the doctors, which in turn told me they didn't expect him to survive.

In cop killings, the underworld is usually on the side of the police, and the slaying of Tong was no exception. The detectives, who had more informers among the criminal population than the police do now, were certain they would soon be tipped off. And they were. Within days Toronto police had the address of the Montreal apartment to which Steve Suchan had fled. He was shot and captured by the Montreal police. Then it was Lennie Jackson's turn. He was cornered in another Montreal apartment by a man from the local holdup squad and two Toronto detectives, Sergeants Bill Thompson and Jack Gillespie. Jack knew Lennie well from the many previous occasions on which he had arrested him.

As in the arrest of Suchan, the capture was preceded by a gunfight, which went on until Jackson ran out of ammunition. Anne Jackson, the fugitive's wife, could be heard: "Leonard, give yourself up, give yourself *up*." But he continued to return the three detectives' fire. Gillespie actually got to within a few feet of Jackson, but the closest he came to being hit was when a bullet tore into a door and knocked a wood splinter into his eye. Four of the six shots he fired hit Jackson.

By then, tear gas had been lobbed into the apartment and Gillespie was forced to back out. Anne Jackson, who was pregnant, continued to beg Lennie to give up, pleading, "Len, think of the baby." Perhaps that's what did it. Jackson finally emerged from the apartment, walking behind Anne, who was wearing a bloodstained negligee. Later, at Montreal detective headquarters, she told me she had walked out first to make sure her husband wasn't shot as he surrendered. She had been with Jackson for about four years and had known he was a criminal. "But I love him just the same and always will," she said.

With Suchan and Jackson in hospital, recovering from severe bullet wounds, the only gang members still at large were Boyd and his brother, Norman. They were nabbed almost at once, as a result of a dandy bit of detective work by Payne and his partner, Detective Ken Craven. After the shooting of Tong and Perry, Payne correctly assumed that Boyd would want to get out of town. Payne also assumed that Boyd and his wife, Doreen, would try to sell their small English car before they left. He started watching the classified ads in the newspapers and soon saw one for a car of the right make. Harold Jukes, a morality detective who'd often been used for undercover work because he wasn't as tall as most policemen, was sent to look at the car along with a policewoman posing as his girlfriend. The man they talked to was Norman Boyd. Jukes and the policewoman had a look at the car and left, saying they would think it over. Norman then got into the car and, taking a long roundabout route that was apparently intended to shake off any would-be followers, led Payne and Craven to a house on Heath Street West, near Yonge. Quiet inquiries revealed that a couple resembling Boyd and his wife had, a few days earlier, rented the furnished apartment upstairs. The man had said he was a missionary on his way to a posting in the Caribbean.

The capture was planned for a Saturday morning, starting with a phone call to Boyd, advising him to surrender because there were fifty heavily armed police officers outside, which was no exaggeration. But Payne and Craven managed to spring the lock on the back door with a strip of celluloid. They crept on their hands and knees up the stairs to the apartment, where Boyd, Doreen and Norman were sleeping. Payne remained on his hands and knees, inching over to the bed, where he put the muzzle of his cocked revolver to Boyd's head and said, "It's Payne. Don't move." His partner was covering Norman. At Boyd's bedside was a suitcase containing a loaded gun and $25,000. The sun was hardly up, but Mayor Allan Lamport was there in a flash to congratulate Chief Chisholm and have his picture taken with Boyd and his captors. I missed all this because I was in Montreal, covering Lennie Jackson's capture.

Tong died about a week after the whole gang was behind bars. News of his death was kept from Suchan, lest it adversely affect his recovery. He and Lennie Jackson did recover and were returned to Toronto and locked up in the Don Jail with Boyd and their old pal Willie the Clown, who'd been sent back from Montreal sometime earlier. A sentry box was erected outside the jail and two policemen were always on duty, one remaining in the box while the other circled the building. This was both a precaution to keep the gang in and to keep out any confederates who might try to rescue them.

The Boyd gang story faded out of the newspapers over the summer months. Then, early in the morning of September 8, 1952, the day before Jackson and Suchan were to go on trial for Tong's murder, I got a call at home from the night city editor, who told me to get over to the Don Jail. All available police cars, he said, had been sent there in response to what the police dispatcher had enigmatically described as "trouble."

When I arrived, I found the place ringed by uniformed policemen. An inspector told me that the Boyd Gang had got out of their cells, and it was believed they had climbed up to the roof. The fire department had sent aerial trucks, and cops were at the top of the tall ladders, sweeping the roof with spotlights. The two sentries who'd been stationed outside the jail, taking turns walking around it like strike pickets, insisted that no one could have got by them without being seen. Inside, the place was being thoroughly searched, while the prisoners were having a grand time, hurling insults through the bars at the police outside. "Where's Lamport?" one yelled. "He's only in on the captures," another shouted, and a third prisoner called, "Hey, you flatfeet, they're not here, they're gone." The inspector turned to me and said, "I think he's right."

Boyd, Suchan and the two Jacksons had been lodged in four isolated cells that opened onto a short hall. No one ever explained how, but they had acquired, or had made, keys to their cells and had been creeping out at night to saw through the double set of bars in the window at the end of the hall with hacksaw blades, camouflaging the cuts with blackened soap. The reason for the confusion on the morning of September 8 was that the hole in the bars was very small and no one could believe they had gone through it. Therefore, the official reasoning went, they must be hiding in the building or on the roof.

Outside, the Keystone Kops scenario continued until one of the sentries finally recalled hearing a flock of roosting starlings suddenly take off at about five a.m., which was well before dawn and something the birds had never done before. Therefore, the official thinkers concluded, the gang must be gone, but even then it was still a while before the hunt shifted to the Don Valley. About three miles north, police found some railway workers who had seen a man with one leg being helped along by others. This, of course, was Lennie Jackson, who had fled without his artificial foot. The confusion and delay was such that after passing the railway men,

Lennie was able to leave the other three and, wearing a tin can over his stump, go to his wife's apartment on Howard Street, near Bloor and Parliament. He visited with Anne and their new baby, put on a spare artificial foot and left one minute before detectives Jack Gillespie and Bill Bolton arrived at the apartment door.

The next day, *every* story on the front page of the *Star* was about the escape, the postmortems on how it could have happened and public demands for heads to roll. Premier Leslie Frost ordered a royal commission to look into the matter, and the governor of the jail, the deputy governor and the staff who'd been on duty that night were suspended, for there were officials who still thought the hole in the bars was too small and were wondering if someone at the jail had let the gang out through the back door. That was not the case. As was later proven, the four men had indeed gone through the little hole.

Of course, there was considerable public interest in the Boyd Gang and the Tong murder trial to begin with, but we turned the escape into an even greater sensation than it was. The reason for this was that the story broke during our latest circulation battle with the *Telegram*, and for the first few days after the breakout, the two papers seemed to be locked in a contest to see which could print the biggest headline. On day two of the escape, for example, we ran photos of the four desperadoes under a huge head that read DEAD OR ALIVE — $26,000. Even Doreen Boyd got into the act, calling Gordon Sinclair at radio CFRB and saying the gang planned to rob four banks a day. By the end of the week, however, the public was sick of it, and Hindmarsh ordered us to lay off unless we had something real to report.

So there followed a couple of days of nothing, not even a bank robbery, which gave the cops the idea the gang was long gone from Toronto. Then, in the early morning of September 16, the story came screaming back into the headlines. In Scarborough Township, just to the east of the city, Constable Andy Ouellette tried to stop a car bearing a license plate that was bent up so the numbers couldn't be read. The car accelerated. Ouellette gave chase and someone in the other car tore his windshield out with machine-gun fire. He emptied his pistol at the fleeing car before crashing into a ditch. I pounced on the incident with a speculative story about how Ouellette may have stumbled onto the Boyd Gang and they had tried to do what they'd done to Tong and Perry.

Media coverage of the incident provoked the usual flurry of alleged sightings that police get in such cases. They don't mind getting them, because every now and then one pays off. One did in the hunt for the Boyd Gang. On the afternoon of the sixteenth, the chauffeur for a Toronto businessman who lived on a big spread north of the city phoned the North York Township Police to report seeing some men hanging around a neighbor's barn. Sergeant Maurice Richardson and Detective Bert Trotter went over to check it out. It would be hard to say who was more surprised by the result, the two detectives, or Boyd, Lennie and Willie, who had no chance to grab the guns they had stashed in the hay. They were handcuffed and taken to the police station, protesting that they had no idea where Suchan had gone.

Three constables were sent to search the barn for firearms. Only luck saved them from suffering the same fate as Tong. As they walked in, they heard a clicking sound in the hayloft. They looked up and found themselves looking at Steve Suchan and the muzzle of an automatic pistol. He was trying very hard to kill them, but his gun had jammed. Even as the three constables watched, Suchan tried a couple more times to get a shot off, then the cops had him covered. Suchan disgustedly threw the jammed pistol into the hay.

That night, there was a regular media circus, as the small but extremely proud North York police force showed off its catch. They even allowed reporters to stand outside the cells and interview the prisoners, which is very seldom done in Canada, and it resulted in a first for Canadian television. That night, the CBC's Toronto station, which had only recently gone on the air, ran in-jail film footage of Boyd and the others, along with a report by a fledgling newsman named Harry Rasky, who later won fame for his series of remarkable documentaries.

When I talked to Boyd in his cell, he pretended to be concerned about a report he'd heard of a policeman being shot
that morning. He meant the attempt to kill Ouellette, and I
wondered how he could have known about it, since the gang
had no radio in the barn. The most likely theory was that the
gang had heard about the Ouellette incident from the guys
with the machine gun. It had happened on a side road that
could lead to the barn, and the police came to believe that
Constable Ouellette had accidentally intercepted a shipment
of guns to the gang's hideout.

Seldom have the Toronto courts acted so quickly. The day
after they were caught, Suchan and Lennie Jackson were
standing before Chief Justice James McRuer, a stern judge
who had prosecuted murderers before he was sent to the
bench. John J. Robinette had been retained by Suchan, and
another excellent criminal lawyer, Arthur Maloney, acted for
Jackson. At one point, the lawyers argued that the fact that
Suchan and Jackson had used a mannequin for target practice should not be allowed as evidence that they had
planned all along to kill anyone who tried to arrest them.
Chief Justice McRuer disagreed. In less than two weeks, the
jury returned a guilty verdict and a date with the hangman
was set.

The killers were now back in the cells they had escaped
from, this time with guards standing right outside. But even
with all the beefed-up security, things were still tense inside
the old walls of the Don Jail. More hacksaw blades were
found on a window sill by Inspector Frank Kelly of the OPP
and Detective Sergeant Bernard Simmonds of the Toronto
police, who were preparing a report for the royal commission that was trying to determine how the gang had got out
of what the public had been assured were escape-proof cells.
Kelly and Simmonds also found more sawn bars. But no matter who had cut what, the central fact was that the jail was
very old, built long before there was such a thing as saw-re-
sistant steel, and cutting through the bars was like going
through butter. "Well, almost," Boyd told me.

He had been sentenced to life in prison by the time
Suchan and Jackson were executed. They both spoke sneer-

ingly of Boyd, whom they regarded as a coward, afraid to face police gunfire the way they had done before they were captured. But as brave as Suchan and Jackson professed to be, they were two shaken men when jail authorities surprised them at midnight and told them everything was ready. Previous hangings in the Don Jail had always been at eight in the morning. The hangman was a plump, jolly Montrealer who wore a beret. As he was about to put the hood over Jackson's head, Lennie turned to him and asked, "Does it hurt?"

"You won't feel a thing," the executioner assured him.

Boyd served twelve years, was paroled and went on to live a quiet, exemplary life, out of the limelight, somewhere on the west coast. About the only thing I ever heard about him after his parole was the surprise visit he paid one day to Adolphus Payne, who was suffering from Parkinson's disease and had retired to Port Hope, Ontario. When Payne was buried, many felt that Boyd would have liked to attend his funeral, but realized that it would put him back in the news, which he didn't want.

For a newsman, the days of the Boyd Gang were not only exciting but lucrative. The American Newspaper Guild, the reporters' union, was by then entrenched at the *Star*, and if you spent all night hanging around outside jails and chasing about the countryside, you were paid overtime, which had been unthinkable in the thirties and forties. In the early fifties, my usual pay was $100 a week. The night and day I spent on the final capture of the Boyd Gang resulted in a cheque for that one week of $464 net.

After the gang had been put away, one of the banks threw a swanky party at the Royal York for the Toronto and North York police who had been involved in their capture. The main reason I remember it is that I had just stopped drinking and was under considerable pressure to start again at the party. It was hard to do, but I kept my resolve. I mention this because, except for the bottle at the Austin Craft hanging and the two drunks at the Lambton Bridge during the Labatt kidnapping, I have not given you any indication of how well lubricated we always were in those days. Part of it was the pressure and long hours of the job. Also, there was booze at press conferences and virtually everywhere else you went. Looking back now, it was truly a totally different era. Nobody, for instance, was thinking about how *unsafe* it might be to drive a car home. And I always did get home in time to get a fresh shirt to wear to the office, and I never missed a day of work. Then, in the fall of 1952, I got a very bad case of sciatica. It laid me up for a month and, I think, saved me from eventually losing my job and perhaps my life. The doctor, who was a strict teetotaler, said booze attacks your nerves and the sciatic is the biggest one in your body. I was by then feeling utterly wretched, clearly under attack from something, so I took his words to heart and didn't have another drink for some twenty-seven years.

18

The Day I Met Igor Gouzenko

IT TOOK A LIBEL SUIT AGAINST ME and the *Toronto Star* to set the scene for my strange get-together with Igor Gouzenko in 1953, eight years after he had fled the Soviet Embassy in Ottawa to expose a network of NKVD spies in Canada.

There was no handshake at our meeting, just a nod each, as we sat across a table to go through a legal necessity called examination for discovery. It is imposed in civil actions, usually at Osgoode Hall, the seat of the law courts in Ontario. This examination, however, was held secretly, in a Toronto hotel suite under conditions that made it hard to believe I was fighting a libel action and not enmeshed in a spy novel.

I had not written anything about Gouzenko at the time he defected. He had been a cipher clerk in the embassy and escaped with a briefcase bulging with copies of NKVD dispatches detailing the information they were getting from their Canadian dupes and spies. The spies included some fairly well-known names, the most prominent of which was Fred Rose, a Communist member of the House of Commons for a Montreal riding. All very interesting, but I was a crime reporter in Toronto, and the Gouzenko case was an international story centered in Ottawa, something I read about in the papers.

Over the years, I had heard from various senior RCMP officers that Gouzenko was a very difficult man to get along with. I thought nothing of it, though, until the summer of 1953, when Lee Belland, the *Star*'s municipal reporter, got some inside information while weekending at the cottage of Mayor Allan Lamport. Another guest was Robert Forsythe, a senior County Court judge and one of three guardians appointed by the federal government to oversee Gouzenko's welfare. For even though it had been almost a decade since his defection, Gouzenko was still living a clandestine existence with the most stringent police surveillance.

And that wasn't without reason. The NKVD (and its successor, the KGB) wanted to kill Gouzenko even after the trials of the spies as an object lesson to others who might consider betraying them. Kim Philby, the longtime Soviet double agent inside the British Secret Intelligence Service, admitted before his death in 1988 that Gouzenko was a disaster to the KGB, but because the Mounties guarded him so well, they never came close to setting him up for the kill.

If Gouzenko was grateful for the elaborate measures taken to keep him alive, he didn't show it. As Lee Belland learned that weekend, there was a serious difference of opinion between him and the RCMP. He called them worse than spies and objected to one of his Mountie guards posing as a boarder in his home. He wanted to go where he wanted, buy whatever he wished and, in general, live better than he could afford on what the government paid him each month. He constantly agitated for more money, and the RCMP often got bills for merchandise he had bought and charged to them.

That was bad enough, but the trouble really mounted when Gouzenko gave the *Chicago Tribune* a series of interviews about Soviet spies operating in the United States. At the time, the hottest thing on television was Senator Joseph McCarthy's sensational investigation of un-American activities. In short, a witch-hunt was on, and not only by McCarthy and his committee. There was also the Jenner Committee, which was bent on flushing Communists out of U.S. government agencies. Both committees wanted Gouzenko to tell them about the spy rings he had mentioned in the *Chicago Tribune* interviews, but Ottawa was adamantly against allowing him to leave Canada. Not only were they worried about his safety, but Gouzenko had by then exhausted his supply of factual information and was not above fabricating spies to maintain his keepers' interest, so there was no telling what he might say before the American TV cameras.

When Belland returned from his weekend, he sent a confidential memo to the city editor, outlining what he had learned, and I was assigned to the story. One of my sources was George McClellan, who later became the RCMP commissioner. At the time, he was head of the Criminal Investigation Branch in O Division, which covered most of southern Ontario and was responsible for Gouzenko's safety. I knew McClellan well because the CIB was part of my beat and I called him every morning. I also talked to other contacts, including members of the Toronto Police Special Branch, who said Gouzenko was a pain in the ass. Everyone I talked to confirmed that the Gouzenko situation was as bad as Judge Forsythe had said, and the city editor told me it was time the public knew about it.

My front-page story appeared October 30, 1953, under a double column headline. It began: "Having gone through $100,000 in high living, Igor Gouzenko, the Soviet cipher clerk who informed on a spy ring eight years ago, is now giving his guardians a headache." In the next paragraph, Judge Forsythe was quoted anonymously as saying, "He appears overanxious to talk, and for money will say just about anything, whether fact or not." It was a good, punchy story, the first honest portrait of Gouzenko ever printed. He retaliated almost at once, with his lawyers slapping a libel suit on me and the *Star*.

Thus, I became the first of the many journalists that Gouzenko would sue over the next thirty years. The only defense in libel actions is to prove that what you have said about someone is true. Newsmen fear such suits, however, because they usually entail demands that the reporter divulge his sources. I had promised my contacts "No names, no pack drill," which they understood. It was a promise I had no intention of breaking. On the other hand, I didn't want to go to jail for remaining silent, and I spent many sleepless nights wondering how I would respond to a demand to reveal where I had obtained the story.

Alexander Stark, the *Star*'s legal counsel and a director of the company, assured me there was no thought of settling with Gouzenko out of court. In apparent proof of this, the paper hired Thomas N. Phelan, one of Canada's most able trial lawyers and an expert on libel cases, to defend us. But civil actions drag on for years before they come to trial, and I all but forgot Gouzenko's suit in the everyday rush to cover the news.

Then, one summer morning in 1954, Phelan called. "I have to meet you, but I can't tell you why until we get to where we're going, wherever that is," he said.

It sounded crazy, but I met him on a downtown street corner, and within minutes we were accosted by a stranger. As soon as he was satisfied we were who we said we were, he pinned a small flower on each of our coat lapels and told us to go to the King Edward Hotel, which was a short distance away. "Sit in the lobby, and the man who speaks to you will know who you are by the flowers," said the stranger, undoubtedly one of Gouzenko's special RCMP guards.

As we walked to the hotel, Phelan told me about the examination for discovery and, several times, warned me to volunteer no information. I was to answer the questions as tersely as possible and only after he had given me the nod to proceed. I got the impression he was afraid I would ramble on and wreck everything.

The man we met in the hotel lobby took us to an elevator, which a house security officer made sure carried only the three of us. A decade after he had spilled the beans on the spies, Gouzenko was still being guarded more closely than a banana republic dictator — by the very Mounties he despised.

We were taken to a sixth-floor room, which was set up with a long table. A court shorthand reporter sat at one end of it, with the lawyers on either side and Gouzenko and me facing each other. At first, I wasn't sure the pale, round-faced man was him. No picture had ever been published, but when he started answering the routine questions that touched on my story in the *Star*, I realized it could be no one else.

I was still worried. I had made up my mind not to say a word about my sources, regardless of the consequences, but I could still see other avenues of disaster. For instance, if records were subpoenaed, that memo from Belland might be revealed and cause a lot of trouble for Forsythe, among others. But it was really the lawyers' show, with Gouzenko and me there just to answer simple questions as simply as possible. When I was finally asked where I had got my story, I said, "I am not prepared to answer that," and that was the end of it. The lawyers, I figured, were saving the rough stuff for the trial, and the meeting ended a half an hour after it had begun.

That was about the last I heard of the matter until early in 1955, when I telephoned Phelan to ask when the trial was expected. He gave me the probable date and said rooms had been booked at the Royal York for the witnesses they were bringing in from Ottawa and Chicago. Apparently, a great effort had been made to check out the truth of what Gouzenko had told the Chicago paper and find people who could confirm what I had written. Phelan was full of ginger, obviously looking forward to cross-examining Gouzenko. "That should be good," he assured me. "We're really going to make them look sick."

As the trial date approached, Borden Spears, the city editor, made plans for cameramen to stake out every entrance to the court. We were going to get a picture of Gouzenko, even if he arrived with his customary pillowcase hood on, no matter which door he used. Reporters were assigned to cover the trial, and I think virtually everyone on the paper was looking forward to the coming battle. In the excitement, I had even stopped worrying too much about what I would have to do when I was asked to betray my sources.

Then, the day before we were to go to court, only minutes before a copy boy brought the first edition up from the press room, Spears called me aside and, with unrestrained bitterness, said, "We're eating crow. You won't like what you're going read, but that's it. Forget the Gouzenko case."

The boy brought in the first edition. On the front page was a double column headline saying, THE STAR EXPRESSES ITS APOLOGY TO IGOR GOUZENKO. And beneath it, exactly where my original story had appeared, were these words: "The Toronto Star, after careful investigation, is now satisfied as to the untruth as well as the unfairness of the report. The Star willingly publishes this complete retraction of the article and expresses its apologies to Mr. Gouzenko for its reflection upon his character and for the embarrassment it must have caused. Mr. Gouzenko has proven that he is a good Canadian. His latest recognition is the winning of the coveted Governor-General's Award. The Toronto Star wishes him continued success in the future."

An *apology*? I was shocked. Then I was angry. I felt I'd been used. They'd given me Belland's memo and used me to deflate Gouzenko and neatly stepped aside when I got burned. The apology didn't mention my name at all, which was a small mercy. But the *Telegram*, always ready to take a dig at the *Star*, ran the apology on their front page and did use my name. That made me angrier.

Phelan, who was very disappointed, later told me that he did not agree with the settlement, but Stark had recommended they pay Gouzenko's $4,000 legal fees and print the retraction. Stark tried to mollify me with a rather sensible explanation of what had gone on. Gouzenko, he said, had not wanted to go to court, and the *Star* had been swayed in favor of an out-of-court settlement by fear that the jury might see him as a poor soul being trampled on by a big newspaper and award fabulous damages to him. Yet I was still the reporter who had been called a liar on the front page of his newspaper, without even a word of warning beforehand. But newsmen, especially at the *Star*, were supposed to be hardened to such happenings. The paper seldom backed up its man. Get the news any way you can, but stay out of trouble. That was the way it worked.

My bitterness didn't last too long, however. Within days, I was informed that my exposé of the Lakehead highways scam had won me my second National Newspaper Award. And shortly after that, as we happened to be walking toward the washroom together one day, Hindmarsh put an arm around my shoulder and said, "I'm sorry about that Gouzenko thing, but I think we deflated him a bit." Then he gave me a raise of twenty dollars a week, or $36,400 over my remaining thirty-five years at the paper. The *Star* was like that. It could stab and then pat your back all in the same week, and you learned to live with it.

I didn't have anything to do with Gouzenko again until June 1982, when a police friend called to ask me to verify his death. He said someone had told him that Gouzenko's demise had been the subject of a radio commentary. I asked around, and neither the *Star* nor the radio station CFRB, for which I was freelancing police reports from headquarters, had heard anything about Gouzenko dying. Eventually I traced the report back to a commentary on CJCL by Barbara Amiel, a Toronto *Sun* columnist. She had devoted her five-minute spot to Gouzenko's life in Canada, his bravery in exposing the spies and said he was being buried that afternoon. She had got her information from Peter Worthington, the *Sun*'s editor, who was Gouzenko's closest newspaper friend. He didn't talk to anyone in the media unless Worthington gave the okay. When Mrs. Gouzenko called Worthington and invited him to attend Igor's funeral that day, he casually mentioned it to Amiel, who decided to give a radio eulogy to Gouzenko.

I passed the tip on to the *Star* and was told they would need official verification before they printed an obituary. The Toronto office of the RCMP said they had long ago ceased guarding Gouzenko and were surprised to hear he had died. An RCMP superintendent in Ottawa who handled media queries was also unaware of Gouzenko's death, but said he would try to confirm it. He called back to say Gouzenko had been secretly buried in a cemetery outside Toronto. He did not say where, and asked me not to say so if I did find out, because there were still radical elements who might desecrate his grave.

In scoring exclusive newspaper stories, the pendulum sometimes swings in your favor and sometimes against. This time it swung in the *Star*'s favor. We had the only picture of Gouzenko ever taken by a news photographer. Bob Olsen got it outside the courthouse building on University Avenue on June 6, 1975. Ray Timson, then the city editor, had assigned Olsen to stake out the court building after being tipped off that Gouzenko and his wife were appearing there daily in yet another civil action. When Olsen stepped from the shadows and snapped Igor's picture, Mrs. Gouzenko charged him, swinging her purse, and Olsen had had to run through the rose garden in order to escape her wrath. The *Star* later received a telephone call from a court official, warning that the picture had been taken on court property. Whether this meant anything legally is doubtful, but the *Star*'s publisher, Beland Honderich, decided against using either the photograph or the sketches of Gouzenko that Duncan MacPherson, the cartoonist, had been making inside the courtroom. There was still fear that Gouzenko might be killed by someone with a grudge, even though it was now thirty years since he'd exposed the spy ring. The photo was kept in a safe in Honderich's office until the day we got the tip that Gouzenko was dead. That afternoon, in a neat little scoop of the *Sun*, the *Star* finally ran the picture, along with a short item announcing his death. It was too close to deadline to write anything more elaborate, but the next day's paper carried several columns about Gouzenko's life. I don't think he would have objected to a single word of them.

19

The Blood of Marion McDowell

THE ABDUCTION OF MARION McDOWELL, which I covered for ten months beginning on the night of December 3, 1953, blossomed into one of Ontario's most puzzling kidnap cases. The story was fascinating in itself, and the newspaper coverage made it even more so, because it was quickly conscripted to do frontline service in the relentless circulation war between the *Telegram* and the *Star*.

The pressure in the newsrooms of both papers was intense as the editors frantically sought new angles every day and pulled out all the stops to keep alive a mystery they knew the readers were gobbling up. This frenzied rivalry and perpetual scramble for something new, however, ran into a solid brick wall in the form of the nonchalant attitude of the small Scarborough Township police force. That force maintained for a long time that Marion McDowell, a seventeen-year-old girl who'd been reported kidnapped from a local lovers' lane by a hooded gunman, had not been abducted at all. She was, they assured us, probably hiding somewhere or had been murdered by her nineteen-year-old boyfriend, Jimmy Wilson.

Wilson had a nasty seventeen-stitch gash on the back of his head to support his version of the story. He and Marion, he swore, had been parked on Danforth Road, just north of Eglinton Avenue, which was then in farm country and not the busy city intersection it is today. According to Wilson, a hooded man had come along and ordered him out of the car at gunpoint and, after taking his wallet, which contained ten dollars, knocked him out with a blow to the head. When he came to, he said, Marion and his car were gone.

The Scarborough detective force was then led by Harold Adamson, who later became chief of the Metro Toronto police. Wilson struck him and his men as an unconvincing storyteller. They grilled him for hours, watching for the telltale inconsistency, the slipup that would reveal what had really happened. It never came. Wilson later told me the detectives told him straight to his face that he was lying and urged him to tell the truth, because it would be better for him in the long run, as Marion's body was bound to be located sooner or later.

All Wilson could do was repeat his story and insist on his innocence. "Okay," they said, "are you willing to take a lie detector test?" Wilson said he was, which meant they had to drive him to Buffalo, where the police had a polygraph and officers trained in its use. Canadian police did not use this technology. The Scarborough detectives expected Wilson to flunk the test and, realizing he was playing a fool's game, break down and tell them what had happened to Marion. He astounded them by passing with flying colors, and on the way home, they finally said they believed his story.

The detectives' skepticism was, to some extent, understandable, because parts of Wilson's story did have a hollow ring. His wallet was found nearby with blood on it and the ten dollars still in the pocket. He also said that although the blow to his head had knocked him out, he remembered briefly coming to and finding himself lying on top of Marion in the back seat of his car. Then, he said, he lost consciousness again and when he revived, she and the car had vanished. His car, however, was found only a short distance away, a little farther up Danforth Road.

The hunt for Marion drew thousands of volunteers. Even

motorcycle gangs joined in. And this is as good a place as any to introduce yet another element of the story, which eventually gave it a significance that took it beyond newspaper headlines and the McDowell family's dreadful tragedy. At the time, there were thirteen municipalities in what is now Metro Toronto. Each had its own police force and they rarely told one another anything about what was happening on their turf. For instance, around that time in Forest Hill Village, where many wealthy people lived, homes were being broken into and large amounts of jewelry taken. The thieves were pawning their loot hardly three miles away, in downtown Toronto, but the Forest Hill police had not said a word about the thefts to the Toronto police. Similarly, the search for Marion McDowell got off to a slow start because the Scarborough police bungled the case in a number of ways, not the least of which was failing to immediately alert neighboring forces about the possible kidnapping.

Even after the hunt for Marion began, the police were still hoping to find that she and Jimmy Wilson had pulled a stunt so she could live away from her parents, although her relationship with them was a very good one. They could provide no leads. Neither could her friends. Her fellow employees at a downtown Toronto photo engraving firm, where she had worked as a typist, were questioned, but none of them knew anything about her friends or what she did in her hours away from the office.

Sick pranksters soon got into the act. Marion's family started receiving tormenting telephone calls. First they would hear a woman's screams, then a man would come on the line and say he was going to kill their daughter. Another sicko called with a $50,000 ransom demand, instructing the McDowells to insert a message in the *Star* classifieds when they had raised the money. We couldn't help but scoop the *Tely* on that one, but it proved to be only the latest of the many false leads we frantically pursued. Hardly a day went by when we *didn't* go on a wild goose chase. For example, one morning a woman called me from Minden, Ontario, saying she had definite information about Marion and could draw me a map of where the police would find her body. I told the city editor it sounded like a pipe dream. He agreed, but fear that the *Tely* might get the tip if we didn't follow it up overruled common sense, and I raced up to Minden with photographer Paul Smith. The woman had not had a pipe dream. A few nights before, she had attended a seance and the medium had told her where Marion lay dead. The woman gave me a map the medium had drawn, showing stone pillars near Lake Ontario. I tossed it out the car window as Paul and I raced back to the chase in Toronto.

But with nothing substantial to report, even we could not keep it up forever, and the story began to run out of steam and looked as though it might fade away altogether. Then one morning, I went out to a house in the east end to cover a murder. I arrived just as the coroner was leaving. He said a woman had been strangled but wouldn't give me her name because the homicide detectives were still trying to find her husband to tell him his bride of a few months was dead. A neighbor told me the woman's name was Norma Schreiber and that she'd worked at the photo engraving firm with Marion McDowell. That brought the case back to the front pages, and one of our reporters, who had interviewed Norma at work, tracked down the photo studio that had done her wedding pictures. The *Star* bought the negatives and ran a different shot every day for about a week, until the police charged Norma's husband with her murder and announced that there was no connection between it and Marion McDowell's disappearance. After that, the McDowell case pretty well faded away until the summer, when the *Telegram* suddenly devastated us with an announcement that it had hired the famous Inspector Fabian of Scotland Yard to find the missing girl. Fabian was really a retired Yard man who had made a name for himself catching jewel thieves and written a book about it. The British press had taken to paying him handsomely to give his views on current crimes, and one paper had actually hired him to look into the case of a missing woman. The publicity generated a rash of tips and the woman had been found. One of the *Tely* staff, a former Fleet Street reporter, suggested to the editor that bringing Fabian to Toronto would be a good circulation booster and might just help find Marion McDowell.

As I have said, the Fabian news was a great blow to the *Star*. Now, you may think all this chasing around after scoops was simply a lot of sitcom nonsense, and in many cases you would be right, but it was a deadly serious business to us. Increased circulation meant many millions of dollars in advertising revenue to our employers, and we were under constant pressure to get more people to buy the paper. Also, as reporters, we were truly at war with the *Telegram*, and any time we got beat by them it hurt. Fabian, we knew, was not a murder investigator. But we also knew that the hoopla surrounding his visit would flood the police and the *Tely* with tips, and there was always a chance that one would lead them to the kidnapped girl. Therefore, the prospect of a picture of Inspector Fabian and Marion McDowell appearing on our rival's front page was a distinct possibility. As the crime reporter, I felt particular pressure to come up with something that would deflate Fabian's impact. And I did it.

To explain how, I must go back a bit. As I have noted, the Scarborough police had bungled the initial investigation. Consequently, the attorney general, Dana Porter, had ordered the OPP to take over the case. Inspector Harold Graham of the CIB, who later solved many of Ontario's biggest crimes, was assigned to the job, and he and Inspector Norm Brickell of Scarborough started from scratch and began following the cold, months-old trail they hoped would eventually lead to the solution of the mystery. The announcement that Fabian was on his way to help infuriated them and many other police officers. The police decided that the best course would be to treat the Englishman as any other media person and refuse to allow him to see any information that had not yet been made public. However, John Bassett, the publisher of the *Telegram*, was a great friend of Leslie Frost's Conservative government, and Porter ordered that Fabian was to get full cooperation and be shown every bit of information the police had. Graham and Brickell were enraged, but knew better than to protest publicly.

The night Fabian arrived, I got a call at home from a voice I didn't recognize. "Don't ask who's speaking," the man told me. "If you want to get the real McDowell story, talk to Noble Sharpe. Ask him what his report says about the back seat of Wilson's car."

Noble Sharpe was a doctor, "the blood man" at the provincial forensic sciences laboratory. Normally, if I asked him anything, he would just tell me to talk to the officer handling the case. When I got in touch with him after that phone call, however, he seemed neither surprised nor reticent, which led me to suspect that higher ups had told him to be nice to Jocko this time. Also, he was as ticked off as anyone else about Fabian's interference. And what he had to tell me was an absolute bombshell. You see, until then, we and the *Tely* had been writing all our stories from the angle that Marion McDowell could very well still be alive, held against her will by the abductor or even forced into prostitution by what was then known as a white slavery ring. But Sharpe told me there was no way she could be alive. She had bled profusely on the back seat of Wilson's car, and no one could lose that much blood and live.

Fabian had arrived believing that he would be searching for a live missing person. He would have learned otherwise as soon as he saw Sharpe's report, but he read it first in my story in the *Star* the next day. It completely deflated him and the *Telegram*. He did stay around to fulfill his contract, and the *Tely* reported that he interviewed seventy-four people and got almost six hundred letters and more than nine hundred telephone calls. I know for sure that many of the calls were phony, because they came from the Press Club and sent him haring off in response to all sorts of imaginary sightings. His departure from Toronto was nothing like his arrival. The *Tely* carried no story telling their readers he'd gone, and I learned from a Toronto police source he had flown back to London on an airline ticket bought under another name.

Despite their orders, the police had not shown Fabian everything. But his trip to Toronto and the headlines it generated got him a better assignment. He was engaged to write a daily column on the trial of Dr. Sam Shepherd of Cleveland, who was charged with the murder of his wife. I read Fabian's comments with dismay. Even he must have been shocked at how much he could get away with saying without fear of being in contempt of court. Nevertheless he had a field day, his opinions weighted on the side of the DA, who was arguing that Shepherd, and not a burglar, had killed his wife. In one column Fabian said a defense witness had shifty eyes, which was a clear indication that he was a liar. If such comments appeared in a Canadian or English newspaper, the publisher would go to jail. But Fabian's columns ran in scores of U.S. papers. Shepherd was found guilty, but eventually freed by United States Supreme Court, which ruled that he had been the victim of hysterical headlines and comment that undermined the right of the jury to make up its own mind whether defense witnesses were telling the truth.

The *Telegram* produced figures to show that the Fabian stunt produced sixty thousand new subscribers. Few of these stayed with the paper. Marion McDowell's body was never found and her death remains a mystery. But it did leave one lasting legacy. Dana Porter later told me that the mishandling of the case was one of the key considerations in the provincial government's decision to amalgamate the thirteen municipal forces into one metropolitan force.

20

The Case of the Missing Bridge

INVESTIGATIVE REPORTING wasn't my usual work. I didn't have any particular liking for it, and I had never been very successful in breaking a story that meant that kind of meticulous reporting. The Highways Department scandal of 1954, however, was a marvelous exception and won me my second National Newspaper Award.

It began just after the new year, with a phone call from an accountant who had once worked at the *Star* and was now an auditor with the provincial government. I was peripherally aware that four men were about to go on trial in Fort William (now part of Thunder Bay) for defrauding the Highways Department of $25,000. Three of the accused were small trucking contractors and the fourth had been an employee of a large road-building firm. The provincial auditors had caught them in a swindle that involved charging the government for hauling loads of earth and rock that hadn't been hauled. The auditors had also uncovered evidence of even greater corruption, but had been told to back off because it would embarrass Premier Leslie Frost's government. This angered the auditors, and one or more of them had decided to tip the press that the four men going on trial were just the fall guys and that several large-scale, well-connected officials of road-building firms were being protected.

I learned most of this only later. During our telephone conversation, the accountant didn't tell me much beyond the fact that the fraud was not a matter of $25,000. *Millions* of dollars had been stolen, and if I went up to Fort William and dug around, I would hear all about it. I wrote a story based on what the accountant had told me and showed it to Borden Spears, the city editor, who said I should get up there.

My first story was little more than a bare statement that auditors were looking into certain discrepancies pertaining to road-building contracts that amounted to more than a million dollars, which was huge money in those days. The roads in question were all in northwestern Ontario and included a part of the new Trans-Canada Highway. The story was immediately denied by the government and its friend, the *Globe and Mail*. But when I got to Fort William with photographer Paul Smith, I didn't have to poke around very long before realizing that I was on the right track.

The trial of the four men was soon to start, and two of their lawyers made a point of asking where I was staying, the clear implication being that someone would be getting in touch. At the accountant's suggestion, I went to nearby Kakabeka Falls and talked to a Highways Department employee, who was too afraid to say much, but he did reveal the sort of questions the auditors had been asking, which gave me an idea of what road-building costs should be looked into. And one evening, in my room at the Royal Edward Hotel, I got a call from someone who suggested I investigate the matter of a bridge that was supposed to have been built on Highway 17. The government had paid for it, he said, but the auditors couldn't find it anywhere.

The missing bridge made a dandy story, and the paper ran it. But I got a call from Tommy Lytle, the *Star's* news editor, who said, "Listen, Jocko, Queen's Park says your stories are all bullshit." I assured him they weren't and asked him to leave me up there. I still didn't know who was doing the swindle or *how* it was being done, but I was pretty confident I soon would, because by then I had got a call from someone who said he would be coming around with that very information. Shortly after Lytle's call, the guy called again and said, "Don't leave the hotel." That day I smoked twelve cigars, waiting for him. He didn't show till the next day.

This was Donald Gandier, one of the four men who were on trial. He said he was broke and wanted to know how much the *Star* would pay for his story. The government, he said, was putting the blocks to him and the other three and he needed $1,500 to pay his legal fees. I was skeptical. I had seen occasions where someone had been paid for a tip and delivered nothing. And although it sometimes paid for exclusive stories, the paper had never approved of checkbook journalism. So I told Gandier it wasn't up to me. I'd have to give the paper a pretty good idea of what it would be getting, before it parted with that kind of money. He said he could tell me how the major contractors were cheating the government out of millions of dollars, and if the story ever got out, criminal charges would be inevitable.

I called Toronto and outlined what he had told me. The man did have a great story to tell and it had to be told. But another consideration also came into play. Joseph E. Atkinson had died in 1948, leaving the *Star* to a charitable foundation as a way of avoiding death duties. For whatever reason, the government objected to this and had passed retroactive legislation that enabled it to take control of the paper. In short, the provincial government had seized the *Star*, and we were in no mood to let any opportunity to take a whack at Frost and his boys slip by.

Gandier's money was wired to Fort William in two lots, one via CP, the other by CN. I cashed them at different banks, gave him the cash and then spent the whole night in my hotel room, listening and taking notes as he explained in detail how the highways swindle was accomplished. They did it with pencils and erasers. That is, before a road is built, the engineers prepare a graphlike profile of the terrain over which it is to go. Up at the Lakehead the contractors and some government engineers were getting together and erasing parts of the actual terrain and drawing in rock barriers where only earth faced the bulldozers, hills where no hills had existed before, imaginary swamps where there was actually firm ground, and fictitious gullies that would have to be spanned by fictitious bridges.

The contractors would then bill the government for the cost overruns they said they had incurred by this unexpectedly difficult terrain. But the plot was even more insidious than that. You see, in those days, one of the main sources of the government party's election campaign funds was companies doing business with the Department of Natural Resources and the Department of Highways, and some pretty funny things went on. In this case, as Gandier and several other sources told me, these road builders got the contracts by bidding extremely low on the jobs, knowing full well that no one was going to look too hard at their subsequent cost overruns — as long as they were generous to the Conservatives at election time.

The story was one of the biggest ever to appear under my byline, and the day after it was printed, I got a telegram from the assistant managing editor, Harry A. Hindmarsh (son of Harry C.), saying, YOU ARE A HERO. EVEN SINCLAIR SPENT 10 MINUTES TODAY SAYING HOW MUCH HE LOVES YOU. In other words, Gordon Sinclair had devoted his radio broadcast to my story. And the other papers, including the *Globe*, jumped on it, too. The government could no longer brush the matter aside, and Premier Frost, speaking in that homespun manner he had, said, "If they're in it, they're for it," and announced an all-out probe by Woods Gordon, a Toronto accounting firm. As the uproar continued, the OPP was directed to open an investigation, and Charles Dubin (who later conducted the Ben Johnson inquiry and is now Chief Justice of the Ontario Supreme Court) was appointed a special prosecutor.

The Liberal opposition wanted a royal commission, as well, which would have really got to the bottom of things. But the government did not want *all* of its dirty linen made public, so it referred the issue to a select committee of the legislature, instead. In May 1954, it was officially reported that 212 contracts had been diddled to a tune of $15,705,557.07, and several contractors and Highways Department employees were arrested and charged with conspiracy to defraud the government.

I went up to Fort William to cover the trial in October, shortly after Hurricane Hazel hit Toronto. I had packed for a long stay, but on the train, a man from the attorney general's office said we wouldn't be there for more than a day.

"How can we be there only a day?" I asked rather sharply.

"You'll see," he said.

He was right. The trial lasted forty-five minutes. A deal had been made, by which the contractors' *companies*, not the contractors, would plead guilty and be fined $250,000. The word around the Lakehead was that the contractors had made it plain that if they went to jail, they would blow the whistle on the whole scheme and take a lot of good Conservatives with them. So, since you can't send a corporation to jail, it was arranged for the companies to take the rap. The government engineers pleaded guilty to charges of breach of trust and were given fines, but no jail sentences.

The only people who went to jail out of all this were Donald Gandier and the other three men. They were sentenced to spend the better part of a year in Guelph Reformatory, and the government was bent on seeing they served their full terms, without the time off for good behavior they were entitled to. I wrote some stories about this scandal, and Gandier and the others and their friends were writing to the federal justice minister, Stuart Garson, pointing out what the contractors and engineers had got away with. The federal (Liberal) government finally intervened, and three of the men were freed about three weeks before their full terms would have been up. The fourth had already served his term and been released.

The Fort William scandal brought me many tips on road-building irregularities all over the province, and for a while there it looked as though I was the Highways Department correspondent and not the crime reporter. In one story, for instance, I revealed why hundreds of thousands of dollars were having to be spent repairing mysterious cave-ins on the 401 near Belleville. As my informant explained it, one of the big headaches in building roads in southern Ontario was getting rid of large tree stumps. The customary way was for the contractors to pay farmers to allow them to put the stumps on their property. In the Belleville area, the farmers didn't want the stumps. So they had been buried in the roadbed and were now rotting, with the highway collapsing on top of them.

Another tip sent me to North Bay and yet another scandal, which properly should have been another big scoop, coming so soon as it did on the heels of the Fort William affair. In this case, I learned, one of the most beautiful homes in the North Bay area was a large cedar-log house overlooking Lake Nipissing. The owner was the Nipissing District Crown attorney, A. C. Alcot Tilley, who had built the place very cheaply. He had got the prime cedar logs free from the Highways Department depot in Sturgeon Falls, and most of the construction had been done by off-duty OPP officers.

The OPP regulations were very strict: officers were not to work at any other jobs while they were members of the force. But, one of the first lessons young officers learned was that they could scarcely make a move without the district Crown attorney's permission — this man was God. Tilley did pay the officers for their work, and no doubt some were glad of the extra money and the chance to get in good with the Crown attorney, but the ones I talked to were angry about having been tacitly shanghaied into doing this work for the man who was, in effect, their boss. Moreover, the radio equipment in the trunk of one of their cruisers had, at no little cost, been damaged while hauling stone for Tilley's magnificent fireplace.

It wasn't the greatest story I had ever uncovered, but it was a good one, and the office had been quite enthusiastic about it when I got the tip. I didn't expect another YOU ARE A HERO telegram, but when I sent my piece down to Toronto, I had every reason to expect it to appear under big headlines on the front page. It didn't appear at all. Nor did I hear from the office. In those days, you didn't question things. You didn't phone the city editor and demand to know *why* a story had been killed, so it was a couple of days before I called the office and reminded them that I was still in North Bay. "Yeah, well, you better come home" was the response. When I did get back, I asked what had happened to the story. They clammed right up, and it took a while to find out what was going on. What was happening was that the powers that be at the *Star* had begun negotiating with the government for the return of the paper to their hands. The government was already mad enough about the Fort William scandal, and it had been decided not to antagonize them further with one from North Bay.

21

The Plot to Kidnap
Marilyn Bell

IN THE MID-FIFTIES, THE FIERCE COMPETITION between the *Tely* and the *Star* gave rise to a brief, frantic period in which somebody always seemed to be trying to swim across Lake Ontario to Toronto. The *Tely* was very keen on the sport, and their usual practice was to secretly slip a swimmer into the water at night and then announce in its first edition that So-and-so was already halfway across. It became a joke around our newsroom, with people saying, "Who's in the water now?" and "Where's the latest swimmer?"

It all began in 1954, when the CNE hired Florence Chadwick, the record-breaking English Channel swimmer, to cross the lake on September 9. The *Tely* got behind the event and, in effect, made her their swimmer. Not to be outdone, Harry A. Hindmarsh decided that the *Star* would sponsor Marilyn Bell, a sixteen-year-old local girl and a pupil of the famous swim coach Gus Ryder. The idea was for Marilyn to enter the water at the same time Chadwick did and make a race of it.

Chadwick was the world's greatest female marathon swimmer and a household name virtually everywhere in Europe and America. No one doubted that she would leave Marilyn Bell far behind. But for some reason, Chadwick could not make it across Lake Ontario and had to drop out of the race, beaten by a young girl who was hardly known outside the Toronto area. It was a stunning sensation, and tens of thousands of people rushed down to the lakeshore.

Marilyn was supposed to land at the breakwall off the Exhibition grounds, but she got tired and started to zigzag. Nobody could now predict where she might land, and the crowd swarmed back and forth along the water's edge in the dark, hoping to be in the right spot when the brave girl arrived. As it happened, Marilyn came ashore at the seawall to the east of the Ex, right in front of Ted Dinsmore, a photographer who was freelancing for the *Tely*, and he got the picture that was shown around the world. The exhausted girl was put aboard a harbor police boat and taken to their station at the foot of Rees Street, about where the SkyDome is now. With her were Gus Ryder and George Bryant, a *Star* reporter-photographer who had been in the boat that had accompanied her across the lake.

Shortly afterward, I got a call at home from the office, telling me to get down to the harbor police station and stop the *Tely* from kidnapping our swimmer. When I got there, Jack Gale, another *Star* reporter, showed me an ambulance that was parked nearby. It looked innocuous enough, but Alexandrine Gibb, who'd accompanied me to my first big swim twenty years earlier, had noticed that one of the attendants who had arrived with it was Dorothy Howarth, a *Tely* reporter, dressed up as a nurse. This nurse had disappeared as soon as she was spotted, but two other attendants had taken a stretcher into the station.

Apparently, when Marilyn was ready to be moved, the ambulance was going to come screaming up to the door and spirit her away. I put a stop to that by yanking the ambulance's distributor cap off and throwing it as hard as I could into the darkness. As I later heard, when it had become obvious that Marilyn Bell, who was under exclusive contract to the *Star*, was on her way to pulling the sports upset of the decade, the *Tely* had suffered a collective fit of sorrow and rage. The owner, John Bassett, had heard the news at home and called the managing editor, Doug MacFarlane, a former *Star* employee who hated the paper, and ordered him to get an interview with Marilyn no matter what.

Bedlam is as good a word as any to describe the chaos inside the harbor police station. Marilyn was in a back room, being guarded from the mob of *Tely* reporters and cameramen, who were trying to convince the harbor cops that they had as much right to talk to and photograph the heroine as anyone else. Moreover, they had got Mayor Allan Lamport down there to help them. I don't think Lamport had been specifically asked to try his hand at kidnapping. The *Tely* had been the only paper to support him during his election bid, and I suspect that he had simply been invited down to get his picture taken with the new swimming star. Maybe the idea was that the harbor cops would be reluctant to keep the mayor (who was also chairman of the police commission) away from Marilyn. Or maybe it was thought it'd be easier to get her into the ambulance if the mayor was beside her.

I indignantly told Lamport about the planned abduction and said Marilyn Bell was under contract to us. She was *our* swimmer and no one else had any right to photograph or speak to her. Lamport accepted this and backed off. So did the harbor police. But there was still the problem of getting Marilyn to the suite we had reserved for her at the Royal York Hotel. Outside, I could hear the engine grinding as someone attempted to start the ambulance, but who knew what other foul plans the *Tely* had up its sleeve? The office solved that one by hiring its own ambulance and summoning every available Diamond taxi to surround the vehicle and escort it to a rear door of the hotel. In the suite, Marilyn was examined by a doctor and went promptly to sleep. I stayed there the whole night and most of the morning, fending off the steady procession of reporters and magazine writers who came to the door under various pretexts, asking to speak to the girl. One of these was young June Callwood, who said she was working for *Maclean's*, which was then a monthly, so any story she wrote would not appear until well after we had run our exclusive. I suspected she had been sent by the *Tely*.

No one else got close to Marilyn, but we were *still* scooped. You see, George Bryant, who'd been with Gus Ryder in the boat, was supposed to interview Marilyn and ghostwrite her personal account of the epic swim. But he had been up for more than a day and had gone to sleep in the suite even before she did; she had been too tired to be interviewed by anyone, anyway. Thus, the next day, while our first edition appeared without an exclusive personal story, the *Tely* came out with one plastered all over its front page. Or so the public thought. The *Tely* did not actually *say* the story was by Marilyn Bell. But they had got a sample of her signature from an old examination paper and put it at the top of the article, so people couldn't help but think these were Marilyn's own words. Later on, the *Tely* got her real signature on a contract, and they had her swimming the English Channel and the Strait of Juan de Fuca. This was all done, of course, to boost their circulation, and it did, at least temporarily, but the *Tely* could never keep the readers it attracted with its stunts. They did not put out as interesting a paper as we did, and that is the primary reason the *Telegram* folded in 1971.

As I have indicated previously, I loved my job and truly resented the few occasions when I had to miss a day because of illness. However, as exciting and as rewarding as I found the work and the competition with the *Tely*, I must add that I did not want my son to be a newsman. Ron did work at the *Star* as a summer replacement reporter while he was going to university, and that was fun, especially on the day in July 1957 when we each had three stories on the front page. Ron had the best one. A man had drowned while at a picnic on Centre Island. Ron had gone to get a picture from his widow, and she told him about how a real estate salesman had accosted her at the funeral parlor and tried to pressure her into using the life insurance money she would be getting to make a down payment on a house. After listening to me at the supper table all those years, Ron knew what was news.

But when he got his BA and announced that he wanted to make news his career, I did everything I could to talk him out of it. There was just no money in it, I argued, and urged him to go to law school. He finally agreed to give it a try for six months, on the understanding that if he didn't like it, I'd see if I could get him a full-time job at the *Star*. That would not have been much of a problem, because Borden Spears was satisfied that he would make a good reporter. At Osgoode Hall, though, Ron fell under the spell of G. Arthur Martin, his criminal law teacher, and forgot about being a newsman. He eventually became a Crown attorney, then went into private practice. Then, on August 22, 1985, we had a small family party at the Skyline Hotel. It was a double celebration. Marjorie and I had been married fifty years, and Ron had just been appointed a District Court judge. In fact, he was the judge in the recent Ernst Zundel hate literature trial. By then, the exciting, occasionally glamorous life of a newsman, which he had heard about from me at home and had seen for himself at the *Star*, had long since become a thing of the past.

That is, although neither I nor probably anyone else could have told Ron this, back in the fifties, when I was trying to discourage him from becoming a reporter, both society and the news business were already beginning to change. The TV crew that showed up at the North York Township jail to film the Boyd Gang was one small sign. Radio was becoming a more aggressive news medium. In short, the whole point and purpose of newspapers was about to undergo a radical transformation that would soon make shenanigans like the Marilyn Bell caper, and the style of reporting that I had been trained in, seem like curiosities from a remote, distant era. Of course, no one could really see it at the time, but the watershed, at least as far as crime reporting went, was the Peter Woodcock case, which came along in 1958.

Sometime before Woodcock actually entered the picture, a young boy was found dead at the CNE. The police concluded that he had been killed accidentally while horsing around with some other kids. However, a young coroner named Morton Shulman pointed out that human excrement had been found near the body, which was consistent with the behavior of a certain twisted type of murderer. The police did not accept his theory, and Shulman got into a fierce wrangle in the newspapers with John Nimmo, then the acting chief of detectives, who continued to insist that the cause of death had been "horseplay." This was, I believe, Shulman's first major appearance on the public stage. He stuck to his guns, and the police eventually charged a boy with the murder. The boy was tried in juvenile court and sentenced to an indefinite term.

Not long afterward, a little girl was found murdered under the Bloor viaduct. Something about the case reminded Detective Jim Crawford of a boy who had been caught molesting girls in North York and let off with a reprimand. This was Peter Woodcock, who was now seventeen years old. He insisted that he'd had nothing to do with the murder until Crawford, who later became head of the homicide squad, decided to seize his bicycle and compare the unusual tire tread with that found near the murder scene. Woodcock then confessed to that murder, the murder of a child at Cherry Beach *and* the murder of the boy at the CNE to homicide detectives George Sellar and Dick Gibson. His account of the crimes included details that could only have been known to the murderer and the police.

The fact that an innocent boy had been sent to prison for the CNE killing was bad enough, but I soon learned that the authorities were in no hurry to let him out. I suppose they were reluctant to publicly admit their error, which was understandable, but every day that the boy remained in jail only heightened the injustice. One morning, I called a Crown attorney named Henry Bull at home to tell him that we had the story and ask some questions. He flew into a rage and said I would go to jail if we printed anything about it. He did have some legal justification, in that it was juvenile matter and thus under strict reporting prohibitions. But it was also an enormous wrong and the public had every right to know about it. Borden Spears, the city editor, agreed with me. Moreover, he said I should use the innocent boy's name in my story, which was unquestionably illegal. And as for Bull's threat to jail us, Spears said, "If you're talking to him again, tell him we'll welcome any action he takes against us."

In other words, we were not going to let the authorities hide their mistakes behind the Juvenile Delinquency Act.

The story ran with the boy's name, but we heard nothing further about going to jail. Yet, even with all the publicity, the boy still wasn't released. That only happened after his family hired Patrick Hartt, who was then one of the province's promising young lawyers and is now a justice of the Ontario Supreme Court. After a tough fight, he finally won an official admission that his clients' son was innocent. As for Woodcock, a Supreme Court jury found him not guilty for reasons of insanity. He was sent to what was then called the Ontario Hospital for the Criminally Insane at Penetanguishene. He is still there.

Now, so far in my account of this case, I have given you only the good side of the media coin: in watching for and exposing official malfeasance, the media are at their finest, and this is one of their fundamental roles in our society. But the other side of the coin is that they sometimes go overboard, which was what we did in the Woodcock case. Normally, we were very careful to word our crime stories so that, although we occasionally came close, we never actually came right out and said an accused person was guilty of the crime that he or she had been charged with. When Peter Woodcock was arrested, however, the *Star* and the *Tely* were engaged in a particularly intense circulation battle, and all caution and common sense were thrown out the window. For several days, both papers ran the story under giant headlines, and every word and every picture we chose to use implied that Woodcock was guilty.

Not long afterward, the Ontario branch of the Canadian Bar Association discussed the matter at its annual conference. As more than one speaker pointed out, they were not only bothered by stories that had, for example, quoted neighbors as saying Woodcock had always been a strange, troublesome boy. The very size, wording and positioning of our headlines, and the big half-page pictures we had run, had amounted to a trial in the press. Woodcock *was* clearly guilty. But in cases where the accused person's guilt was not so cut and dried, a similar trial in the press would preclude a fair trial in the courts.

As a result of that discussion, Chief Justice James McRuer

had a quiet word with all the newspaper owners, making it very plain that, in future, the courts would be watching closely for anything resembling the Peter Woodcock circus, and any paper foolish enough to try a similar display would be immediately nailed for contempt. The *Star* was now run by Joseph S. Atkinson, the son of the founder, who didn't care for crime news in the first place. So all of a sudden, the *Star* just stopped using crime to sell papers. I still had to keep track of what was going on and write it up, but my stories, even very big ones that would have got tremendous play only a few months earlier, were now put below the fold on the front page, or hidden inside the paper or ignored entirely. It was a disheartening time to be a crime reporter.

Things loosened up a bit when we saw that the *Tely* was not being nearly so scrupulous as we were, and for a while there, I had hopes that the restrictions were only a temporary measure. But it was never the same again. Looking back, I suppose I was one of the first to be shoved into the new era. Maybe that was why, in 1960, I accepted an offer to freelance reports from police headquarters on radio CFRB, which I did in addition to my work for the *Star*. The odd thing here was that, in later years, Joseph S. Atkinson made a point of telling me how much he enjoyed my broadcasts. He did not appreciate crime in his newspaper, but he liked to hear about it on the radio. As I said, it was a brand-new era.

22

The Death of John Chisholm

AT THE BEGINNING OF THIS BOOK, I said John Chisholm was the greatest police chief Toronto is ever likely to see. I did not mean he was a man without flaws. He was egotistical, though not in a brazen way. As an administrator, his habit of promoting only men who had been through the detective ranks to the position of divisional inspector, one of the prized jobs in the department, created a lot of dissatisfaction in the uniformed force. And although he was a friendly, often jolly man, people were afraid of him. In the end, he had no friend who dared tell him to his face that he was headed for disaster, and all anyone could do was stand back and watch with amazement as he disintegrated.

An ascetic Dundee Scot, John Chisholm had been a meticulous, sometimes spectacular, working detective. One day, for example, while driving to the office, he spotted a man who was wanted for armed robberies all over Canada and the U.S. walking along College Street, near Dovercourt Road. Chisholm pulled to the curb and got out of the car with his pistol drawn. The robber ducked behind a power pole and opened fire. Chisholm stood there, holding his ground and trading shots with the man until he wounded him.

As chief of detectives, one of the first things he did was insist that his men wear clean shirts every day. Many of them were bachelors, and in those days, single men saved on laundry bills by wearing rubber dickies — synthetic shirt fronts that usually looked quite awful. Chisholm also insisted they wear fedoras. But he didn't just want his men to *look* good. His goal was a first-rate detective force, which meant they had to prepare their cases so meticulously that they had a ninety-five percent chance of standing up in court. The detectives had to report to him daily, even those on duty in the divisional offices; and if a team was working on a big case, they had to see him even more frequently, keeping him up-to-date on their progress.

During the Draper era, he was, as I have said, the real brains of the police department. When he became chief, he quickly moved to make the entire force his own. He kept the divisional inspectors on their toes with unexpected phone calls, and if they didn't have prompt answers to his questions, he immediately wanted to know why. The desk sergeants at the various police stations scattered around the city soon got used to looking up from their work to find the chief standing there, checking things out in person.

Chisholm's usual routine was to put in a full day at headquarters, have dinner with his family, then go for a workout at the west end YMCA and return to his office. From there, he would go out on his surprise inspection tours or catch up on his paperwork; and if he had to deliver a speech, he would practice it for hours in front of a mirror. His vanity demanded that he look good, but he also felt that making a good impression on people helped to raise the esteem of the police force in the eyes of the public. In the same vein, his wife used to tell other women that "Jack" wouldn't let her wear makeup because he believed the chief of police's wife had to be very plain in dress and manner. He was, in short, a Scot of the old school.

But the new Toronto was emerging.

In 1953, the Metro government was created, amalgamating many of the thirteen municipalities' services, though not their police departments. The chairman of the new Metro Council was a Conservative party bagman named Fred Gardiner, who had been appointed to the job by his great friend and political ally, Premier Leslie Frost. If you wanted, say, a hotel beverage license, it was wise to make a donation to the Tory party, and Big Daddy, as Gardiner was called, was the man to see about it. He had also been a high-powered criminal lawyer, with some very shady characters, including Manny Feder and the other big gambling interests, among his clients.

About 1955, in the wake of the Marion McDowell case, Metro Council formed a committee to study the amalgamation of the thirteen police forces. The chairman was Charles O. (Bob) Bick, an optician, the reeve of Forest Hill Village and a great friend of Big Daddy Gardiner. The committee recommended amalgamation and, in 1956, at Gardiner's behest, Bick was named the full-time chairman of the police commission. Chisholm, of course, was named chief of the expanded force, which officially came into being on January 1, 1957.

I think a lot of the trouble that followed stemmed from the term "full-time," which was never defined precisely. Previously the mayor had automatically been the chairman of the Toronto Police Commission, which had met every couple of weeks and rarely ever interfered with the chief. Bick, on the other hand, interpreted full-time to mean that he was to be an active chairman every day, not just the guy with the gavel at the formal commission meetings. He moved into an office in the old York County Court building on Adelaide Street East and soon began behaving like an American police commissioner, breezily summoning the chief down from headquarters to discuss various matters whenever he deemed it necessary.

Chisholm, who despised and distrusted politicians to begin with, was perplexed. In 1956 and 1957, he asked me several times to ask Roy Greenaway, who was then the *Star*'s Queen's Park correspondent and a confidant of Premier Frost, to ask him exactly what Bick's powers were supposed to be. Not letting on that the question came from Chisholm, Roy raised the matter with Frost a number of times and always got the same answer: Bick was only the full-time chairman of the police commission. I have always interpreted this to mean that Bick was to be a traditional type of chairman until someone said otherwise, and that no one originally intended him to assume the role he created for himself.

Now, I am not at all blaming Bick for what happened. In fact, he completely threw himself into the task of putting the Metropolitan Toronto Police Force together, giving up his optical business in the process, and he deserves a lot of credit for the work he did. Moreover, amalgamation of the thirteen forces was not purely an administrative matter of melding the thirteen organizations. It was also a highly political job, in that the petty politicians whose turf was now being swallowed up by Metro had got used to being fawned upon and driven around in police cars by their cops. Some of them still wanted out of amalgamation, and after the united force hit the streets at the start of 1957, they frequently made the news by screaming that nobody in the outlying areas saw a police car any more and citizens were being left unprotected. That was why the Metro police cars were painted yellow — so nobody could miss seeing one when it went by.

With many similar external political fires to tend to, Bick did have a tough job on his hands, and he was quickly becoming impatient with Chisholm. I think the heart of the matter was that Chisholm figured that if he had been made chief of the new force, he should be allowed to put it together his way. He resented being buzzed down to Bick's office for instructions. As a result, Chisholm didn't really throw himself into the detailed work of amalgamating the various departments. Bick later told me he was always asking for progress reports on different matters and never getting them. Chisholm, who never called him "Mr. Bick," would say, "Yes, your worship, it'll be ready for you in a few days." It never was. And as Bick also told me, if it had not been for Deputy Chief Eddie Dunn, who took over the administrative work, the new force would never have got off the ground.

As far as I know, Chisholm never confided in anybody, but I suspect that he was procrastinating because he also felt that Bick should be concerned only with policy matters and had no right to see the reports. At any rate, Chisholm did not interfere with Dunn's preparation and presentation of the reports, and the new administration came together almost despite him. Then, toward the end of 1957, everyone began noticing that Chisholm, who normally walked smartly with a stiff, washboard back, had begun to droop. If he saw you coming, he would straighten up, but if you turned around after he had gone by, you would see that he was drooping again.

And I must say here that I contributed to his droop. Early in 1958, while going over to the blotter one day, I noticed that the holdup squad had arrested three men for a series of gas station robberies in Etobicoke. The odd thing was that three other young men had already confessed to these robberies and had been sent to prison. I asked Inspector Bill Bolton, the head of the holdup squad, what was going on. He said, "Don't say *I* said anything, but we got the right guys. You better ask somebody else about the other ones." I said, "You mean, they got the wrong guys and they're in jail?" He said yes, the guys his men had arrested had admitted everything; the detectives out in Etobicoke had got the wrong ones. But, I asked, how could that be? The three guys in Etobicoke had also confessed to the holdups. He didn't say it in so many words, but his answer implied that the Etobicoke youths had been tortured into confessing.

I passed the tip on to the office and Joe Scanlon started digging into the records and interviewing people right away. The result was a tremendous scoop on the *Tely*, complete with interviews with the young men's families and lawyers, who all claimed that they had indeed been beaten into confessing to crimes they hadn't committed. Three detectives were subsequently charged under the Police Act, and the Metro Police Commission launched an extensive investigation.

Chisholm was visibly rocked by the scandal. At about the same time, he suffered an attack of the virulent Asian flu that was going around that year. When he returned to work, I mentioned to him that the flu had got me, too, and it had left me feeling quite depressed for a while. He said he was still feeling that, but he supposed it would go away in time. As far as I could see, it never did. The jolly side of his personality completely disappeared, and he began to behave very strangely.

From his days as chief of detectives onward, Chisholm had always been friendly with reporters and a steady source of news. If a story was about to break, his way of announcing it was to say to us, "Keep in touch." That was understood to mean: "Don't go far away, or call frequently. Something interesting is about to happen." However, although he liked and obtained good publicity, he had never been known as an avid newspaper reader and almost never commented on what we wrote about the department, whether good or bad.

Then, early in 1958, about the time of the Etobicoke scandal and his bout with the flu, he suddenly became obsessed with newspapers. Every night, around nine o'clock, he would get his driver, Tommy Constable, to take him down to the *Globe*. At the time, it was the only morning newspaper. However, the first, or "bulldog," edition of the next day's paper was printed at about nine in the evening, mainly for street sales to people interested in race results. The *Globe* building was then at York and King streets. One wall of the press room was a mass of windows and you could stand out on the sidewalk and watch the paper being printed. That's what Chisholm started to do, with his nose pressed to the glass. Then, when the papers were ready, he would hurry around to the back door, buy a copy from the first newsboy to emerge and return to his car, where he would study the paper page by page. When he was done, he would fold it up and say, "Okay, Tommy, let's go home."

About eleven o'clock the next morning, he would send Tommy out for the first editions of the *Star* and the *Tely* and pore over them in the same manner. It was later surmised that he was searching for a story or a hint that he was about to be fired. By then, Bick and other members of the commission had noticed his weariness and were imploring him to take a boat trip to Scotland with Mrs. Chisholm. He always replied that he would think it over, or that he might do it later. Of course, if he was already afraid of being removed from his job, he must have interpreted these pleas for him to go away for a while as a plot to get him out of the country while someone else was put in his place. I am certain there was no such plot. Nor was what happened next part of a larger plot, but I am sure that it, more than anything, contributed to the demise of John Chisholm.

In the spring of 1958, Big Daddy planted a story with Alden Baker of the *Globe* that, at a meeting of the police commission to be held the following day, he was going to demand that Chief Chisholm fully account for a secret and illegal police department fund that had come to his attention. The Metro treasurer, Big Daddy added, was unaware of this fund; and as he understood it, the chief used it for lavish entertaining.

Gardiner was right about one thing: the Metro treasurer was in fact unaware of the fund, and it was illegal under provincial regulations. But it was not a secret to anyone who knew anything about the police department. Everyone called it the Stool Pigeon Fund, and it had existed for decades. It worked this way. Each year, the police commission allocated $25,000 to the fund, and this sum, plus money from the regular auctions of unclaimed bicycles and such, was used to pay informers, pay rewards and to entertain visiting dignitaries. The accounts were kept in a ledger that was stored in the headquarters orderly room. Chisholm was notoriously frugal with this money, and on the rare occasions he felt it necessary to take visitors to lunch, they never went to a licensed restaurant. It was almost always the Round Room in the Eaton's store that used to be at College and Yonge, where the luncheon special cost $1.50.

The whole thing could have been cleared up with a couple of phone calls, but Big Daddy was a headline hound. His story in the *Globe* dripped with innuendo that there was monumental skulduggery afoot, and he vowed to get hold of the secret ledger and demand an accounting for every penny spent. Accordingly, at the commission meeting, he began by demanding to see the ledger. Chisholm was reluctant to hand it over for a number of reasons. Above all, this was the record of police payments to stool pigeons, which nobody should see, because informers tend to get beaten or killed when the criminal element finds out what they are up to. Also, Chisholm regarded Gardiner as one of the great un-hanged crooks, and I suspect that among the entries in the ledger were the names of people who had informed on Big Daddy's clients.

Chisholm had the ledger with him, wrapped in brown paper. He unwrapped it, saying he was prepared to answer all questions, but he had an obligation to keep the informers' names secret. Big Daddy reached across the table and tried to grab the book. Chisholm pushed his chair back, out of reach, with a look of extreme fear on his face. He appealed to Bick, to no avail. Apparently Bick felt Gardiner had a right to look at the book to see where the money was being spent.

Bick told Chisholm to give the book to Gardiner. Chisholm did and then dutifully answered a long string of sneering questions about those $1.50 lunches in the Round Room. It was purely a spectacle for the press, and when it was over, Big Daddy probably thought that was the end of the matter, and for him it undoubtedly was. But Chisholm left the room with a terrible expression of fear and defeat on his face.

A few weeks later, Chisholm was scheduled to speak at a testimonial dinner for my old mentor, Charlie Oliver, who was still covering police headquarters for the *Globe*. All the newsmen who gathered at the Prince George Hotel that night noticed that Chisholm had lost weight and had a completely different demeanor. This was simply not the chief they had known for so many years. The testimonial was late in start-ing because Charlie, writing under the name Appas Tappas, also covered the horse races and was still at Woodbine. Chis-holm became very restless and suddenly left. He returned a short time later, and when he found that the dinner still wasn't about to start, he bought a string of liquor tickets and passed them around and went away. If he had taken his pis-tol out and put a shot in the ceiling, he couldn't have shocked us more than he did by buying those liquor tickets and passing them around. It was completely out of character. Only later, when all the pieces were put together, was it real-ized just how badly he was breaking down.

Early in the summer, he had Tommy Constable drive him

to the Lake Simcoe area. At a certain spot, he told Tommy to stop and got out of the car. Without a word about where they were or where he was going, he walked off up a road. A few minutes later, Bick, who was working in the garden at his cottage, looked up to find Chisholm standing there. "Oh, it's you, John," he said. "Yes, your worship. I was just passing by, and I thought I'd drop in." Chisholm stayed for about ten minutes and left. Two weeks later he returned and hung around for two hours. These strange visits, plus letters addressed to Bick but later found in Chisholm's office safe, from both the police force's doctors, urging that Chisholm take a leave of absence because of nervous exhaustion, left the distinct impression that Chisholm had gone up to Bick's cottage to kill him. Bick himself thought this was the case.

Then, on July 3, 1958, Chisholm paid a surprise visit to James Mackey, the inspector in No. 9 Police Station, who had been put in charge of the inquiry into the Etobicoke torture scandal. Chisholm asked him how much longer he expected the investigation to take. They chatted about that matter for a while, then Chisholm suggested they go downstairs to the pistol range and fire a few rounds. This, too, was completely out of character, but you didn't question Chisholm, and Mackey soon found himself engaged in some unscheduled target practice.

The next day, it was raining heavily, so I hung around the *Star* office and worked on the telephone, instead of going over to the city hall court offices, which I generally did every morning before I went to police headquarters. About nine a.m., I got a call from Chisholm, which was a very rare occurrence, though he was always accessible if you needed to call him. "The chief speaking, Jocko," he said. "A special meeting of the board at twelve noon. Keep in touch." The board was his name for the police commission. He hung up before I could ask him any questions.

My immediate reaction was that he must be resigning. Twenty minutes later, he called again and repeated his first message word for word. When I told him he had already called, it seemed to upset him, and he said, "All right, I did," and hung up. After the first call, I'd been reluctant to phone

Bick and ask about the special meeting, for fear that my inquiry would get back to Chisholm. After the second call, I
was sure he was going to quit the force and I had to call Bick.
If Chisholm was indeed going to resign, a story about him
and his colorful police career had to be prepared in advance
and set in type.

But Bick said there was no special meeting, only the one
that was already in progress. They were discussing the
Etobicoke brutality case, which had been put on the agenda
well before today. He also told me that the commission had
noticed the chief's health seemed impaired and had been
trying for some time to get him to take that ocean trip to
Scotland with Mrs. Chisholm. "And," Bick added, "if he does
come in with his resignation, I can tell you it will definitely
not be accepted."

It was still raining heavily at noon, when I heard the police
radio dispatcher urging D-1, the chief of detectives' car, to
call in. He repeated the message several times without an answer. Then he abruptly changed the message to a request for
D-1 to go to High Park at once, and that was followed by a
call to the chief coroner to go there as well. I went over to
Borden Spears and asked him to send Alexandrine Gibb in a
taxi to High Park. He asked why, and I told him about the police calls and said I thought the dead man in the park was
Chisholm and that he had probably killed himself. Spears
looked at me as if I'd gone off my rocker, so I told him about
the two telephone calls. Miss Gibb raced out to the park and
got there before the police had put a cordon around the
scene. Within the hour, she was sobbing on the telephone
that the dead man was in fact John Chisholm, who had been
a friend of hers for many years. He was on the front seat of
his car, his pistol at his side.

It was almost deadline for the first afternoon edition — the
one that was delivered to homes in the Metro area. The
story was a complete scoop, although all we could report
then was that Chief Chisholm had been shot to death in High
Park. Suicide could not be mentioned until an official pro-
nouncement that he had taken his own life. I was saddened
by his death, as he had been very good to me.

23

WELL-ORGANIZED CRIME

CHISHOLM'S SUCCESSOR WAS JAMES MACKEY. He was the most junior inspector, and his promotion jumped him over the heads of three deputy chiefs and all of the divisional inspectors, but Bick had been impressed by the way Mackey had handled the investigation into the brutal questioning by police of the three Etobicoke youths. Mackey got the news at the police field day, while he was raking sand in the broad jump pit. Bick came up and whispered in his ear, "How would you like to be the new chief of police?" Mackey nearly fell over. "Don't you tell a soul," Bick warned. Mackey didn't even tell his wife.

At first, things were quite rosy between the chairman and the new chief, then Mackey's nerves started to go. In 1961, police headquarters moved from College Street to the old Imperial Oil Building at King and Church. Bick ensconced himself in what must have been the corporate top dog's headquarters. This was on the seventh floor. Mackey was on the sixth, and his office was connected to Bick's by a private staircase. Mackey was always running up and down those stairs. His friends began to fear that he would suffer the same fate as Chisholm, and they got him away for an extended vacation in Florida. When he returned, he was a relaxed and changed man, and his differences with Bick seemed to be healed.

Mackey was by no means a weak man. Before he became chief, certain defense lawyers used to call him Mack the Knife. He is the one who solidified the new Metro force and made it into one of the better police organizations anywhere. And, in the early sixties, he had the strength and vision to curtail the Mafia's incursion into Toronto. You can't keep those people out entirely, but you can minimize their influence, which Mackey did by being especially vigilant and creating the necessary intelligence apparatus.

The key man here was Herb Thurston, whom I had known for years. In fact, I was the first person he ever pinched. That was in 1937. Thurston was then just a cadet, having been hired because he was a good pole vaulter (the regular pole vaulter on the Toronto police track-and-field team was getting old and could no longer beat the pole vaulters on the Montreal and Detroit teams). At the time, there was a crackdown on the sale and purchase of cigarettes on Sunday. I knew that, but one Sunday I did buy some in the café under the *Mail and Empire* building, after first having a good look up and down the street. When I came out with my purchase, a skinny cop stepped from behind a telephone pole and put the clutch on me. This was Herb. I still have the summons I got, saying I was charged with a violation of the Consolidated Statutes for Upper Canada, 1859. To wit, contravening an act to prevent the profanation of the Lord's Day. I was fined two dollars.

Thurston went on to bigger things. In the late fifties, he and his partner, Walter Johnston, were the first to warn that organized crime was moving into the city. Many of the senior detectives laughed or just dismissed them as paranoids. But the partners had a special vantage point, in that they were working on the fraudulent manipulation of penny stocks. They knew that Mafia figures were involved and that they were also running a protection racket against shady stock salesmen. It took some effort on their part, but Thurston and Johnston gradually got people to listen to them; and the whole town sat up and took notice in March 1961, when members of the Hamilton Mafia moved in on the gambling empire of a man named Max Bluestein and beat him almost to death with iron bars in the Town Tavern. It was mainly Thurston's work that put Johnny Papalia and two other men in jail for that crime, and he went on to head the Metro police force's organized crime intelligence unit, and then a similar, provincewide unit for the Ontario Police Commission.

But I have got very far ahead of myself, and this chapter is not about the Mafia, anyway, mainly because I had almost nothing to do with them except to write up their rub-outs. This chapter is about gamblers. And to get an idea of the background of what I'm talking about, you might make a note to check the newspapers on the Monday after the next Super Bowl. I am willing to bet you will see that the police arrested a number of bookies over the weekend. Many of them will be people who have been being arrested for bookmaking ever since I was a cub reporter. In other words, despite the big raids of 1938 and so forth, gambling has never been stamped out. All the police can really do is keep a lid on it. However, in the late fifties, the gamblers were getting completely out of hand, and the police were almost powerless to stop them because they were being protected by corrupt officials of the provincial government and a strange quirk in the law.

I got onto the story by following up a tip that Chief Mackey was engaged in a tug-of-war with the provincial secretary's office over the revitalization of dormant club charters, which was at the heart of the racket. It worked this way. Any charter granted to a private club after 1945 contained a provision saying that police and fire marshals could walk in at any time without a search warrant. Therefore, there was no point in setting up an illegal gambling casino in a club with such a charter. However, charters that had been granted *before* 1945 contained no provision for allowing the police and fire officials in at any time. Therefore, if a gambler could get hold of one of these charters and have it hanging on the wall of his club, the police could enter only with a warrant, which meant they first had to get concrete proof there was gambling going on inside, which in turn meant infiltrating the joint and otherwise getting around the club's security measures. Some of these places had steel doors, vicious guard dogs and electrical warning systems, and it was very difficult to get a cop in to take a look. Also, the gamblers seemed to have an endless supply of pre-1945 charters.

For example, one of the charters I wrote about had been granted around 1919 to the Notawa Community Club, a group of First World War veterans in the Collingwood area. About 1930, the members went on to other things and the club ceased to function. However, its charter still existed, lying dormant at Queen's Park. All a gambler had to do in order to revive it was to provide the provincial secretary's office with a phony list of the club officers who had been elected in the years between 1930 and 1959 (therefore "proving" that the club had been functioning continuously since 1919) and pay a small fee. Thus, in 1959, the Notawa Community Club again became a living, breathing legal entity, and its charter was hanging on the wall of a casino on Dundas Street in Toronto.

But that was only part of it. If the police finally did get the proof they needed and raided one of these clubs, the charter was automatically revoked, but that did not stop the gamblers at all. They simply got *another* old charter, hung *it* on the wall, and they were back in business and the police were back where they started. In other words, someone in the provincial secretary's office must have known about the racket. Indeed, the gamblers could not have found so many dormant charters without help from the inside.

But, again, this was only part of the scam. As the subsequent royal commission revealed, the gamblers had a lot of other helpers in the provincial government, as well. Take the case of the Centre Road Club, in what was then known as Toronto Township and is now part of Peel Region. According to its charter, the members of the club were aviation buffs who liked to gather at the clubhouse to watch the planes flying in and out of Toronto airport. A harmless enough pursuit, but as the OPP and township police were quick to notice, the members thought it necessary to equip their building with steel doors and have attack dogs patrolling the grounds. Moreover, few people were ever around in the daylight hours when aircraft were visible. The club came to life only at night, and surveillance of the place revealed that many of the visitors were well-known gamblers and provincial officials, some of whom had the nerve to arrive in chauffeur-driven government cars.

The police tried to get the provincial secretary to revoke the charter, but were told it could not be done because the Centre Road Club was a branch of the Army and Navy clubs and thus had a *federal* charter. The federal government was eventually persuaded to revoke the charter, and the club was immediately provided with a provincial one.

At one point, the OPP antigambling squad thought it had enough evidence for a raid, and two detectives went to see the Peel County Crown attorney, Grenville Davis, father of the future Ontario premier. During the meeting, he took a call from the attorney general's office; when he hung up, he told the detectives that their evidence wasn't good enough. Davis later told the royal commission that the call had concerned an entirely different matter.

My stories on the charter scam appeared in December 1959, getting big play on the front page. This was rather unusual, because Atkinson was a truly reticent man with a genuine dislike for such unpleasantness. I can only guess that the articles were featured so prominently because we were in the Christmas doldrums and not much else was happening.

As far as the effect of the stories went, nothing spectacular happened for two years. But I was later told that I was the one who got the ball rolling. You see, policemen are generally afraid of politicians. Mackey was always leery about letting politicians get too close to him. And, as I have noted elsewhere, Chisholm despised them, one of the reasons being his firm belief, which he shared with many senior police officers, that the rampant corruption in U.S. police forces stemmed not from the fact that American cops were inherently bad, but that they were functioning in a corrupt political system. The politicians are the ultimate bosses of the police. If they are basically honest, then although there may still be outbreaks of individual police corruption, the police system as a whole will be honest, too.

Politicians were involved in the gambling clubs, so for a long time the OPP and local police departments were reluctant to push the matter. But my stories got tongues wagging. I don't know who was responsible or how it was done, but the Liberals began getting leaks, and John Wintermeyer, the leader of the opposition, started questioning the government about the spread of organized crime in Ontario. Attorney General Kelso Roberts denied there was any such thing, but the leaks and the allegations continued. I helped things along in May 1961 with a story about how Garnet McGill, the chief of the Toronto Township police, had done everything possible to alert the government to the Centre Road Club's flagrant abuse of its charter. In 1959, he had sent photographs, affidavits and other material to the attorney general and the provincial secretary. And, fearing that he would get no action from them, he had also sent copies to Premier Frost's home in Lindsay. The only response he got was a note from Frost saying he would look into the matter. But the club continued to operate at full tilt for another seven months — until December, when my stories appeared and its charter was suddenly revoked.

On November 29, 1961, John Wintermeyer stunned the province by charging that the gambling interests had several high-ranking OPP officers on their payroll. Frost denied it right away. But then, in December, he appointed a royal commission under Mr. Justice Wilfred Roach to look into the matter of organized crime in Ontario. Of course, no politicians or civil servants were tarnished by the ensuing inquiry, but the royal commission did establish that two men named Feely and McDermott, who owned gambling clubs throughout the province, were in fact paying off a number of senior OPP officers. As a result of the investigation, the force got a new commissioner. This was Eric Silk, a senior counsel in the attorney general's office. The first civilian ever to head the OPP, he did a superb job of restoring the force's morale and stature, and the very first thing he did was fire the corrupt officers. One of these was the deputy commissioner who had been tipping off McDermott and Feely about upcoming raids. His name was Jimmy Bartlett. I had first met him some twenty-five years earlier, at Queen's Park, the night he gave me the tip about the J. S. McLean kidnapping.

24

Justice

TWO CASES FROM THE 1960S have stuck in my head for a number of reasons, not the least of which is they are good reminders of the many, sometimes tortuous, ways that justice can be done. One story involved an inquiry undertaken by my friend Harold Graham, a superb detective who was the senior investigator for the Roach Royal Commission on organized crime in Ontario and later succeeded Eric Silk as commissioner of the OPP. The other has to do with me personally.

When I say the Graham story is from the sixties, I mean it came to a climax then. It began shortly after the civic holiday in 1952, when a laborer named Arthur Kendall returned to his farm in the Monkton area. He had been working at a sawmill near Wiarton and living in a cabin at a place called Johnston's Harbour. His wife and five children had gone to stay with him over the holiday. When he returned to the farm, only the five kids were with him, and he had also brought along a former Wiarton waitress named Beatrice Hogue, her six children and all their furniture. The neighbors immediately began asking what had happened to Arthur's wife, Helen. He told them she had thrown a teacup at him one night and stormed out of the cabin, saying she was never coming back. The neighbors didn't believe that for a second. They knew Helen Kendall loved her children, was a caring mother and had endured years of abuse from Arthur to keep the family together. The neighbors did not let the matter rest. Arthur stuck to his story and tried to convince one farmer that Helen was now living with her brother, Ross Cameron, on his farm near Brantford. The farmer telephoned Cameron, who told him that they had not heard from Helen since she sent them a postcard saying she was leaving Johnston's Harbour and returning home. The police were called.

Graham, who was then an inspector working out of the OPP CIB in Toronto, was sent up to investigate the matter with Sergeant Charlie Anderson of the Mount Forest detachment. Kendall told them about the teacup and Helen storming out, adding that she'd been in an ill humor all evening and had refused to cook supper, which was what had caused the fight. However, a local storekeeper who had sold Helen Kendall the food for that night's supper told the investigators that she had been her usual cheerful self. Graham and Anderson were aware that a lot of things could have happened between Helen's visit to the store and dinnertime. There was even a remote possibility that she could have become despondent and taken her own life. But going by what they were hearing from the neighbors, this seemed as unlikely as the notion of her suddenly leaving her kids.

Something about the children didn't ring true, either. So one day, while Kendall wasn't around, Graham and Anderson had another chat with the three oldest ones, Margaret, Anne and Jimmy. Again, they confirmed what their father had said about the fight and their mother storming out. But the detectives saw an entirely different story written on their faces. Each had a look of pure fear, and the cops knew why: Kendall was given to horsewhipping his children and they were mortally afraid of him.

Interviews with people in Wiarton revealed that Kendall was in the habit of telling new acquaintances that he was a widower. The police were now sure he was telling the truth in that respect, and when a box containing a sundress and a copy of the *Farmer's Advocate* with Kendall's name on it was found about a mile from the cabin, they thought they were on the verge of finding Helen's body. Kendall and the oldest children were questioned again. He said no, she had not been wearing that dress when she left, and again, the kids backed him up. Graham led a massive search of the cabin area. It turned up nothing, but he noted in his reports that a nearby swamp contained a patch of quicksand, where a body could disappear forever.

He and Anderson were absolutely certain that Kendall had killed his wife, but they had absolutely nothing to hang a murder charge on. Kendall was kept under watch and taken to court for horsewhipping and injuring Margaret, who was then twelve. A witness told the judge about the vicious beating he had seen Kendall give the child. But Margaret testified that her injuries were the result of a fall and Kendall was let off.

Nine years passed, but neither Anderson nor Graham gave up. Anderson concentrated on winning the trust of Margaret, Anne and Jimmy, periodically dropping in on them when their father was away. Graham kept after Kendall. Whenever he had time, he would drive up from Toronto to wherever the man happened to be working and badger him with more and more questions. He also talked again and again to Helen's relatives and the neighbors, hoping to find the crucial lead.

Kendall must have thought he was safe. His kids were terrified, and perhaps he even believed he could not be charged until his wife's body was found, which is a TV-inspired delusion that a lot of people have. In 1959, Kendall asked the court to declare Helen dead. It did, and he lost no time marrying Beatrice Hogue. He must have been utterly astonished when, in 1961, he was arrested for Helen's murder. By then, he had taken a job as a laborer at the Clinton RCAF base. The night before he was charged, Corporal Harry Sayeau and a Constable Twaddle, both of the OPP, kept watch on the farm with a copy of the warrant in their car, just in case he somehow got wind of what was up and tried to flee. In the morning, they followed Kendall to the base, where Graham and Anderson were waiting to arrest him as he punched in. Graham was already well known around the air base, because that was where, a few years earlier, he had arrested fourteen-year-old Stephen Truscott, accused and later sentenced to hang for the 1959 rape and murder of his twelve-year-old classmate Lynne Harper. When he was charged, Arthur Kendall simply said, "I wouldn't harm a hair on her head." He had been telling the detectives that in those very words for the previous nine years.

But Anderson's patience had paid off. In 1959, Margaret had married and left home. Anne later left to live on her own. Anderson continued visiting them and Jimmy and finally got them to tell him what had happened the night their mother disappeared. They had, they said, been awakened by Helen's scream and saw her pleading with their father, "Arthur, please don't, please don't." Then they saw him draw a knife across her throat. He put the knife on the kitchen table, lifted Helen's body like a sack of flour and carried her out of the cabin. He came back in, wiped the floor and the table and went outside with the bloody rags. The children heard him drive away. He came back a while later, scrubbed the floor and then told them what to say to anyone who asked about their mother.

I have never forgotten the fierce look on Kendall's face as he stood in the prisoner's box in the court at Walkerton, fixing his eyes on his children as they each in turn described the cold-blooded murder of their mother. Beatrice Hogue sat in the row of seats behind Kendall, glaring at them, as well. This was the first trial to be held after Canadian law began making the distinction between capital and noncapital murder. The jury found him guilty of capital murder, but with a recommendation for clemency. This, I knew, would save him from the gallows, and the thought enraged me. Helen Kendall had been slaughtered just like the cows I had seen killed in the abattoir I'd worked in as a boy. Arthur Kendall spent the next fourteen years in jail, except for one short escape, which he spent in the house Beatrice had rented nearby.

It took ten years to arrest and convict Kendall. In 1967, I saw the opposite extreme, when a Toronto man was convicted by a Mexican court in a couple of hours. The case first came to my attention in the form of a brief wire service story that chattered out of the teletype machine on a news-quiet Saturday morning in February. It concerned a woman whose body had been found at the bottom of a sheer precipice overlooking the Pacific Ocean south of Tijuana. After three weeks, the local authorities had, with some help from the FBI and the Los Angeles police, identified her as Margaret Dinino (née Currie) of Toronto. The city editor asked me to see if there was anything in it worth a follow-up.

I asked around headquarters and found a Toronto detective who'd been aware of the case for several weeks. He gave me the background. Shortly before Christmas, Margaret Currie, the forty-eight-year-old daughter of Donald Currie, a prominent man in the dry-cleaning business, had married Stephenino Dinino, who was her junior by twenty-two years. They had left for a honeymoon in Florida in a car leased by the bride, with Margaret promising to call either her father or her stepmother when they arrived. She had not done that. Donald Currie had called the police and been put in touch with the detective, who got him to file a missing person report. Currie had always been suspicious of Dinino, and his doubts about the man and worries about his daughter only increased when, a week or so after he'd reported her missing, Dinino called him from the Western Union office in Los Angeles.

Dinino said he and Margaret needed money, which could be wired to them via Western Union. Currie asked to speak to Margaret. Dinino said she was too ill with a high fever to come to the phone. Currie pretended to believe this and told his son-in-law to stand by, the money would be there in a couple of hours.

As soon as he hung up, Currie called the Toronto detective, who got onto the FBI in Los Angeles and asked them to grab Dinino and question him about his wife. "In any event," the detective added, "we want him in Toronto for skipping bail." Apparently he had skipped bail on a minor assault charge arising from a street fight.

The FBI and Los Angeles police nabbed Dinino at Western Union. With him was a very young woman named Sabina Perez. Despite her youth, she was already the mother of four children and had worked as a hooker and then a barmaid on Constitution Avenue in Tijuana. She seemed genuinely surprised when the police told her that the woman Dinino had called his "old aunt" was actually his wife. Sabina said Dinino was going to marry her. He had even applied for a marriage license, but at the last moment discovered he didn't have the twenty-four dollars to pay for it. Sabina had Margaret's fur coat, her dresses, her jewelry, including her wedding ring, and a copy of her marriage license, but she insisted that Dinino had told her the "old girl" had gone back to Toronto.

When asked about Margaret, Dinino said they had been staying in Mexico at a motel near the ocean and had gone walking hand-in-hand in the moonlight along the top of a cliff. One of her high heels had given way, causing her to lurch out of his grasp and fall screaming over the edge of the cliff. Shortly afterward, Sabina told police, Dinino had come to the roadhouse where she tended bar. He said his aunt had had to leave for home in a hurry. He flashed a roll of money, bought her drinks, asked her to dance and then proposed marriage, telling her he was rich and that she would have a good life with him and her children.

Dinino's story didn't ring true to the Los Angeles or FBI men, but the Tijuana police told them they'd had a body matching Margaret's description in their morgue for almost three weeks. A few hours later, two husky Tijuana detectives arrived in Los Angeles, along with their interpreter, a newspaper reporter named Aurelio Garcia, who covered the police and court beats for a Tijuana paper and was a correspondent for a Spanish-language newspaper in L.A.

A man from the public defender's office visited Dinino to advise him of his rights. He also warned him about going back to Tijuana. "Americans don't get justice as they know it in Mexico, and Canadians can't expect any different," he said. But, citing her possession of the dead woman's effects, the Tijuana police charged Sabina as an accessory to Margaret's murder. As a result, Dinino waived his right to an extradition hearing and voluntarily returned to Mexico, insisting that he loved Sabina and wanted to tell his story so she would be set free.

I went down in May to cover his trial. In a Tijuana jail cell that was so crowded you could hardly raise an arm, Dinino told me that Garcia, the detectives' interpreter, had had a lot to do with his decision to go back to Mexico. He'd assured him that he had nothing to worry about; as soon as the police took down the story of his wife's accident, he and Sabina would be set free. Sabina *was* set free, but not Dinino.

It had not been difficult to get into the Tijuana jail to do the interview. The newsman I used as an interpreter had said all it would take was to make sure the man at the main gate saw the five-dollar bill in my hand. When I arrived, there was a throng of people trying to get in to see friends or relatives. They could not pay the gratuity and had to wait for hours in the smelly corridor. In the few minutes I had to wait, I happened to glance downward to my side and saw a child's face peering out a small cell door not much more than eighteen inches high. It was a holding tank crammed with street urchins who had been caught stealing and were being held until their parents could be found.

When I first talked to him, Dinino was amazingly confident that his court-appointed lawyer would be able to spring him. When I came back a couple of days later, he wasn't quite so sure, though the confidence was still there. He was to make his first appearance in court, and having had some inside experience of the Canadian justice system, he expected there would be a few brief formalities followed by an adjournment. It couldn't be otherwise, he said, because his lawyer had not been in to see him.

He met his lawyer for the first time when he was taken to the so-called courtroom, a cramped space in a cement block building. There was no judge's dais or any other furnishings one expects to see in a court of law. The lawyer could not speak English. Dinino knew no Spanish. There was an interpreter present, but he ignored most of the questions Dinino asked him to put to the lawyer, who really spoke to Dinino only once, telling him through the interpreter to shut up or he would make the judge angry. Dinino did as he was told.

The proceedings began with a reading of the statement Sabina had given to the police. It was translated for Dinino. Several times he indicated that he disagreed with what he was hearing, but a wave of his lawyer's hand was enough to tell him that his objections meant nothing. Further police statements were read, and while the cops were droning on, the judge took to periodically getting up and leaving the room. I followed out of curiosity one time and found him in another room, signing papers for a fee. This, he explained, was how he made his living. He was only hearing the case as a favor to the regular judge, who had gone deep sea fishing.

Finally, after returning from another of his periodic absences, he announced that he had heard enough and that probable guilt had been established by the autopsy report, which stated that Margaret Currie D'Nino (sic) had sustained skull and facial injuries before she fell down the cliff.

With that, the hearing came to an end. "When do I go to court?" Dinino asked the judge. He was told he was already there. "Don't I go before a jury?" No, they said, jury trials are only for federal crimes. Tijuana had more than two hundred murders a year, so juries were out. Dinino was shaken and near tears, as he probably realized for the first time that he stood little chance of defeating Mexican justice. After a finding of probable guilt, the onus falls on the accused to prove, in the period before sentence is passed, that he could possibly be innocent. Dinino was told that this period could be about four months, and he was carted off to La Mesa penitentiary.

Back in Toronto, Dinino's aunt, who had raised him as her own child, began to be hounded night and day by letters and telephone calls from Tijuana lawyers, who claimed to have political clout and said they could get Steve freed for payments ranging from $200 to $5,000. Dinino himself began calling his aunt and me from the penitentiary, with no apparent worries about long distance charges. He could do this, he boasted, because a girl at the local telephone office belonged to a group that visited prisoners on Sundays and had fallen madly in love with him.

Dinino's aunt didn't believe most of the things he told her, but she fully accepted his claim that he had not thrown his bride to her death. A woman of modest means, whose husband had been long out of work because of an extended strike by the building trades, she did her best to send him money for food. Several times he called and told me he was starving to death, because in Mexican prisons, if you don't buy your own food or have it sent in, you just get a weak soup and some hard bread for every meal. I passed his story on to the Canadian Consulate in L.A., and they sent him ten dollars a week until it came time for his sentencing. He got twelve years. About eight years after that, he called me from the Toronto jail, saying he needed bail. I signed the surety, mainly because I felt sorry for his hard-pressed aunt, and I knew that the charge against him, a years-old common assault rap, would probably be chucked out. It was, and a few days later he appeared in the newsroom to shake my hand and boast that he had met and married a Hollywood woman who had a big home, a string of hairdressing salons and lots of money. "I really love her and I'm settled for life," he said. He told his aunt the same thing. Whether it was true or another of his pipe dreams, I don't know. I never saw him again.

25

The Big Fix

REPORTERS LIKE ME, who are kept on a single beat for lengthy periods, will inevitably encounter stories that test their loyalty to their newspapers and their belief in the public's right to know. In my case, I twice had to balance these against my loyalty to my contacts in the police department and the harm the stories could do to the force.

One was the Breathalyzer scam of 1969. The other was the Etobicoke torture scandal of 1958. Both stories resulted in sweeping investigations by the police commission. However, if the truth be told, the force was fortunate that judicial inquiries were not ordered, because these usually delve deeper into the issues and often conclude with recommendations that criminal charges be laid. In the case of the Breathalyzer scam, two of the culprits actually ended up being promoted, while the only person to be really punished was the officer whose evidence formed the basis of the investigation. He had to wait years before he was promoted, and that alone sent a message to the force: don't be on the wrong side of the fence if you expect to go up the ladder.

I first got wind of the story one Friday in November, when the managing editor, Martin Goodman, phoned me at headquarters. Goodman, who was to become president of the *Star* before his untimely death at forty-five, said an anonymous caller had just told him about some secret inquiry going on in the force. The guy hadn't said much, but he had asked why Jocko Thomas hadn't caught on to it. "Just check it out," Goodman said. "It can't be much if you don't know about it."

That was unintentional flattery. All kinds of things can go on in a police force without a person with even the best of connections knowing about them. But Goodman's call did remind me that two inspectors, Bob Bamlett and Cyril Cole, had been taken off their regular duties and were working out of an office just down the hall from the press room. I had asked them what was up, and they had been rather evasive, but I'd thought nothing of it at the time because there were always internal things happening that were really none of my business.

On Monday morning, though, I started asking around and soon found that Bamlett and Cole had been spending a lot of time with a traffic officer named Ian Samuel, who was well known in the force for his one-man war against drunken drivers. His usual tactic was to park his cruiser where he could observe the patrons leaving busy taverns. If one showed signs of drunkenness and drove away in a car, Samuel would follow and nail him. That is, he would take the suspect down to the Central Police Garage on Strachan Avenue, ask that he be given a Breathalyzer test and, if the guy failed, charge him with impaired driving, no excuses accepted. In contrast to almost all other uniformed officers who worked out of specific divisions under divisional inspectors, all of Metro's traffic officers worked out of the Central Garage under the command of their own inspector.

Samuel wouldn't speak to me. But as I gradually pieced the story together, I learned that he had begun to notice that the cases against well-to-do people he had charged were being thrown out of court. He would show up to give evidence, but the officer who gave the Breathalyzer tests, who also had to testify, would not be there. Usually, the excuse was that he had been assigned to some other task that day and could not make it. Another date would be set, and again the Breathalyzer guy wouldn't show, and this would go on until the judge had had enough and threw the case out. Suspecting a racket, Samuel started keeping a record of these occurrences.

In the course of my own investigation, I talked to several Crown attorneys, asking if Bamlett and Cole had been around inquiring about Samuel's cases. They confirmed this and usually added that they and other Crown attorneys had also noticed the curious absences of the Breathalyzer man and were making notes, too. Then I learned about Peter Lott, another traffic officer, who had recently been transferred out of the garage, pending investigation of a charge that he had attempted to shake down a drunken motorist for $500. Apparently, he knew about the Breathalyzer racket and how far up the ladder it went, and he'd been comparing notes with Ian Samuel.

I was told that Lott had gone to Florida and was in the Tampa area with his car and trailer. I went down there and spent a couple of days and hundreds of bucks on taxi fares, going from trailer park to trailer park, trying to find him. I was on the wrong side of Florida, which I learned when the office called and said Lott had been around Jacksonville Beach and was now back in Toronto.

Lott wouldn't speak to me, either. But by Friday, after a week of digging, I pretty well had enough for a solid story and was looking forward to pulling it all together by next Tuesday. However, on Saturday, Goodman called me at home and said he wanted the story on his desk by Monday morning. I have often wondered if that anonymous caller really was anonymous and whether Goodman knew more than he told me. At any rate, we both knew that Lott was threatening to take his case to Morton Shulman, who was then the NDP MPP for High Park. If he did it too soon, it would blow my scoop. And even if he did hold fire, both Goodman and I knew that the very fact that I had been asking questions would have got tongues wagging, and it was only a matter of time before everyone else got onto the story. I had been particularly worried about the *Tely*'s police reporter. He was a friend of Deputy Chief John Murray, the head of the traffic division, and I was surprised that he hadn't popped up with something already.

Anyway, for the rest the 1969 Grey Cup weekend, I worked on the phone at home, double-checking details and confirming various points. Cole refused to say anything to me. Bamlett was a bit more cooperative in that although he didn't volunteer new information, he did confirm what I had. He and Cole were not by any means involved in a cover-up. In fact, Bamlett, who later became chief of detectives, told me at one point that he fully expected to see a royal commission appointed to look into the matter.

On December 1, 1969, my copyright story appeared under the headline POLICE CONSTABLE QUITS, CLAIMS "HIGHER UPS" FREED IMPAIRED DRIVERS. The constable was Lott, who had just resigned. The story caused a sensation at police headquarters, because only a few people had been privy to the secret inquiry. But what really astonished me was how many policemen, rather than being angry at what I had done, wholeheartedly approved of the exposé.

Chief Mackey was angry, but only because I had not interviewed him. My explanation that he'd been off at his cottage and that Goodman had ordered the story right away placated him. Deputy Chief Harold Adamson complained that the story seemed hastily written and also wondered why I had not talked to him. The reason I hadn't was that I didn't know he was involved in the investigation. Thus, the only person who was truly angry with me was Deputy Chief John Murray, who never spoke to me again.

You see, as head of the traffic division, he was responsible for the Central Garage. Moreover, even though he was not named in the story, the highest of the higher ups that Lott was referring to was clearly *him*, and this was why most of the police were pleased to see my story. Murray, who had come up through the ranks with Mackey, was a kind of gray eminence in the force. When he was promoted to deputy chief, he had been the inspector in charge of the Central Garage, and after his promotion, it was noticed that the only people who were promoted to inspector were sergeants who worked at the Central Garage. This, of course, offended the sergeants everywhere else. But more than that, Murray was disliked and distrusted throughout the force, because he was known as a fixer. Very few people believed he was straight.

The Central Garage in those days was like a closed shop, and once an officer got in there, he tended to stay forever. When Murray became a deputy chief, Bick said he had to work at headquarters. Murray resisted the move for as long as he dared. And when he finally did move to headquarters, we noticed that he came in very early in the morning with shoe boxes full of the cards on which the officers at the Central Garage made out their applications for summonses. Much later, I was told on good authority that what Murray did was go through these cards, looking for the names of friends and people he would like to be friends with. Then he would call these people up and, after some chitchat about the speeding charge or whatever the person had got the night before, say something like: "I think in your case, we'll just send you a warning. No summons will be issued." It's difficult to say what Murray got out of all this, though the word was he wasn't above accepting handouts. It's even quite possible that this was simply his way of cultivating the friendship of important people.

The day after my story appeared, rather than waiting for the attorney general to order a judicial inquiry, the police commission announced that it would conduct its own thorough investigation of the matter. In other words, the force was going to investigate itself, and as soon as word of that came down, cops of all ranks, even some at the very top, were telling me off the record that absolutely nothing would come from the inquiry.

It went on well into 1970. When he testified, Ian Samuel began by saying that more officers would have come forward with information if they'd had the greater protection afforded by a royal commission. As it was, anyone who testified was testifying in front of his or her own bosses. His protest was, of course, noted and ignored. Other testimony was contradictory or denied; a lot of people suffered memory lapses; and at one point, two Crown attorneys had to get their own lawyer to impress upon the commission that suggestions that they were not telling the truth about missing police witnesses were, as the lawyer said, "monstrous and bizarre." In the end, as everyone had predicted, nobody got blamed for anything, although the system for handling applications for summonses was eventually changed so that nobody can easily get at them.

Some time after the inquiry, Murray was relieved of his responsibility for the traffic division and given an executive position. The two "higher ups" at the Central Garage that Lott had named went on to receive extraordinarily good promotions, which shocked me and a lot of cops. Constable Samuel, on the other hand, had to wait years before he received a promotion, and that came only after Phil Givens had become chairman of the commission. At the first meeting of the new regime, he was appointed a sergeant. He reached the rank of staff sergeant before retiring to take up a security position in the private sector.

Immediately after my story came out, the *Tely*'s crime reporter, who was also an inspector in the auxiliary police, congratulated me on my scoop. He said he'd heard about the investigation and had been holding back to see what happened. He disappeared from the police beat soon afterwards, and then left newspaper work to become a private investigator. It never occurred to me that my story would merit even a submission for a National Newspaper Award. Goodman kept the news to himself until the day before the 1970 awards were announced, when he told me I had won. It was my third award. René Lévesque was to be the guest speaker at the awards banquet, but became ill at the last minute. I was asked to fill in for him. I have never been shy about such things. And since the topic of investigative reporting was in the air, and because a *Star* executive was at the head table, I decided to tell the story of A. C. Alcot Tilley's beautiful home on the shore of Lake Nipissing and how and why the paper had killed my article about the OPP laborers who'd built it with Highways Department logs.

26

The Politics of Policing

HAVE YOU NOTICED that for the past few chapters this book has been more about politics than crime? One of the reasons is the downplaying of crime stories that, as I've said, began at the *Star* in 1958. Another reason is, although politics have always been part of policing, Toronto is now a much larger, more complex place, and senior police officers today spend as much time on the politics of their jobs as they do on law enforcement. The change came with the creation of the Metro police commission, which essentially made the post of police commission chairman a political plum to be handed out to friends of the provincial government. Bick was the first to benefit from this system, and he was also its first victim. But before I get to the story of how and why he was booted out, I have a couple of other anecdotes about the often convoluted politics of modern policing.

The first concerns the arrest in June 1971 of Harold Ballard and Stafford Smythe for defrauding Maple Leaf Gardens of $487,000. The charges were the end result of a long chain of events that began with the Maple Leafs receiving its share of the Buffalo franchise's NHL entry fee. This initiated a quarrel with the Department of National Revenue over whether the money should be treated as a capital gain, which was not taxable, or as income, which was taxable. The feds of course insisted it was income. Ballard and the others went on maintaining it was a capital gain to the point where the tax authorities were moved to send the RCMP and a squad of chartered accountants into Maple Leaf Gardens to look at the books. The audit uncovered irregularities having to do with renovations to the homes of Smythe and Ballard which had been charged to the Gardens.

The arrests followed a year-long investigation by the Metro fraud squad, which was working under Clay Powell, a special prosecutor in the attorney general's office. The media knew about the investigation almost from the start, but not a word of it was made public. I tried to get the story into the *Star* several times, but was always told that the risk of a libel suit was too great and that I should wait till an arrest had been made. I asked the fraud squad to keep me posted and almost forgot about the case, until Sergeant Lloyd Creighton stuck his head into the press room one day, and said, "Let's go." They were on their way to the Gardens. Nobody ever expected Ballard to go to jail. The word was that he simply had too many good friends at Queen's Park and the fix was in. It must have been a pretty authoritative word, because Powell ended up going to Ottawa to see Justice Minister John Turner. Sources later told me that Turner assured Powell that if there were any interference in his prosecution, the federal government would intervene. Powell never said anything about it, beyond acknowledging that he had seen Turner. Smythe died before the trial started. Ballard was found guilty and served about a year and a half at Millhaven. As this book was being prepared, Clay Powell was acting as the special prosecutor for the Mount Cashel orphanage inquiry in Newfoundland; Ballard's death in April 1990 received front-page headlines, which would have pleased him no end because in life he was always happy to be on the front page, even while he was in the penitentiary.

The other story I mentioned concerns the kidnapping of Marilyn Lastman in January 1973, which was treated with great skepticism by the media. It began seriously enough on the day her husband, Mel Lastman, the newly elected mayor of North York, was to preside over the inaugural meeting of the North York city council. Just after noon, Mrs. Lastman phoned a relative to say a man had called and said Mel had suffered a heart attack and had been rushed down to the new Mount Sinai Hospital. The same man, she added, was going to take her there.

The relative called Lastman's office and was assured that he was in the building. Lastman was told about his wife's call, and his first thought was that she had been kidnapped. The police didn't doubt this was a possibility because he had recently mentioned in a newspaper interview that he was worth $10 million, largely from the sale of his chain of Bad Boy appliance stores.

Lastman's first call was to Bick. Bick buzzed Chief Harold Adamson, who had succeeded Mackey in 1970. Orders went out to the police in North York that there was to be no news leak, but it wasn't long before radio CHUM got a tip. At 8:30 p.m. it reported that Mrs. Lastman had been kidnapped and her abductors were demanding $100,000. Chief Adamson then held a press conference, telling reporters little beyond the one known fact: Mrs. Lastman had called her relative, said she was on her way to Mount Sinai and vanished. A horde of media people, including me, gathered in front of the Lastman home, milling around and asking one another questions. All we knew was that police officers were inside with Mel. At about half past ten, a taxi pulled up and Mrs. Lastman was out of it and into her house so quickly that she was on her way through the front door before anyone realized who she was. Later, a few policemen came out and told us that she was unharmed and had gone to bed.

Actually, she was closeted upstairs with Adamson and her husband. I learned this much later from Jim Morgan, the staff superintendent in North York, which meant he was, in effect, the police chief there. In normal circumstances, Morgan, a solid, no-nonsense cop, would have been in charge of the investigation, but he had been left downstairs, as he put it, twiddling his thumbs on a chesterfield.

Outside, I and many other newsmen concluded that it had all been some weird misunderstanding and left. I went down to the office and wrote a little item about Adamson's press conference and a minifeature on how the police were prepared to handle such emergencies. On the way home, driving up the parkway to Bayview Village, where we had moved in 1961, I heard on the radio that Adamson had come out of the Lastman house and told the reporters who were still there that Marilyn had indeed been kidnapped and had been set free shortly before she got into the taxi. I nearly drove off the road.

Adamson's statement sparked a mystery that was still hitting the front pages two months later, with the police issuing so many statements it was difficult to make head or tail of the sequence of events. One statement, for instance, said Mrs. Lastman had been robbed of $92,000 worth of diamond and emerald rings, which had been in her purse. Another statement said her abductors had given her an injection and told her it was lethal and that unless they were paid $800,000 cash, they would not tell her what the antidote was.

Close on the heels of the statement about the stolen rings came another one saying the rings had been found in a dresser drawer, and a press conference was held at the Lastman home. A microphone was set up in the rec room, and Deputy Chief Bernard Simmonds began by explaining that Mrs. Lastman had been in bed one night and, waking up at three a.m., had gone to a dresser to get her nightgown and found the missing jewelry underneath it. The media had been skeptical about the kidnapping from the beginning, with Gordon Sinclair's broadcasts being particularly scathing. In the rec room there, our doubts must have been written all over our faces, and this was not lost on Adolphus Payne, the chief of detectives, who was also present. When Simmonds was through, someone wondered out loud why Mrs. Lastman had not donned her nightgown *before* she went to bed. Payne overheard this and shouted to Simmonds, "Get back on the mike, Barney. They don't believe you."

Simmonds went through it again.

Lastman was sitting in a corner, tense and obviously upset by our skepticism. At one point, he turned to a CFRB man and said he was sick of hearing what that senile old reporter who should be retired was saying about his wife. "You mean Gord Sinclair?" the CFRB guy asked. Lastman didn't reply directly, contenting himself with some disparaging remarks about reporters being "in a terrible business." ˙

When Payne shouted at Simmonds, he was not being ironic or amusing. He and many other senior officers almost desperately wanted us to accept the kidnapping at face value and run stories to that effect. Payne was in charge of the so-called investigation, and he and the others were always coming up with leads and important developments. But I had observed this man's work for almost forty years and several times called him Canada's greatest detective. In this case, he was no such thing. He was simply going through the motions. His partner, Ernie Gill, was doing the same, and every time we discussed the kidnapping, he loyally recited the party line about the latest leads and so forth; but while he was speaking, Ernie was also rolling his eyes and doing everything but say out loud that it was all bullshit. Any lingering doubts I might have had about the validity of the abduction vanished the day I saw the initial release of the major crime statistics for 1973. According to that document, there had not been one kidnapping in all of Metro throughout the entire year. I asked Adamson about it. He seemed flustered and said it was an oversight. I never got around to checking, but I imagine subsequent releases of the 1973 statistics did list one kidnapping.

As I said, it's all politics now. Bick didn't invent the system, and nothing I say here should be taken as a suggestion that things would have been better or different if someone else had been made commissioner in 1956. If anything, things could have been worse, for Bick threw everything he had into his job and he truly loved it. That was why, in January 1977, his sudden announcement of his resignation came as a complete surprise. The only reason I could think of was his health, but I didn't know him well enough to ask him about it.

Of course, the whole police department started buzzing with speculation about who the next boss was going to be, and I found out right away, although I didn't realize it at the time. A morality sergeant approached me one morning and asked, "Jocko, do you know who's going to be the next commissioner?" I said, "I haven't any idea." He said, "It's gonna be Phil Givens." I said, "What are you *talking* about? Phil Givens is a Liberal." The sergeant said, "Well, I'll bet you five dollars on it, anyway." And I said, "No, I won't bet you anything, because it wouldn't be fair to take your money. Givens is a Liberal, and the Conservative government would never give the job to a Liberal." The sergeant pointed out that Givens had already been on the police commission at one time, and I said, "Yeah, but he was on automatically, because he was mayor of Toronto. He was never that interested in it."

I put the conversation out of my head and went south for my holidays. When I returned, one of the first things I saw in the paper was an item saying a date had been set for a constituency meeting to pick a successor to Phil Givens, the MPP for Armourdale, who had suddenly announced that he would not be running in the next election. Oh, oh, I thought, the morality guy was *right*. So I waited at the top of the stairs for Bick to come in that morning. He got off the elevator, and I said, "Is Phil Givens coming here? Is he getting your job?" His face flared angrily and he said, "Yes! It's that son of a bitch Goodman, but don't *quote* me." I said I wouldn't quote him. But he wouldn't say anything more. He just walked into his office and that was it.

Goodman, I knew, had to be Eddie Goodman, a lawyer and a very powerful man in the Conservative party. I wrote a speculative story that Phil Givens was likely to be the next chairman of the police commission and that the Tories had made a deal with Bick to leave. The story was completely denied. Givens said they had talked to him about it because he'd had experience on the commission, but no decision had been made. The other papers picked up the denials. But about three months later, the announcement came from Queen's Park that Givens had been appointed to the police commission — not as chairman, mind you, because the commission elects the chairman itself. It elected Givens unanimously.

What had happened was that the Tories, who had a minority government at the time, were coming up to an election and hoping to win a majority. Part of their strategy was to persuade a couple of popular Liberal MPPs to step aside, the idea being that the Conservative candidates in those ridings would then have an good chance of beating the Liberals' hastily nominated replacement candidates. To get the popular MPPs to vacate their seats, of course, required offering them each a suitable plum as a reward. One of those plums was the Metropolitan Toronto Police Commission, and the fact that Bick was a solid Tory suddenly became irrelevant and he was persuaded to take a walk. The reason that the morality detective had cottoned onto it some four months in advance was that his wife patronized the same hairdressing salon as Phil Givens's wife, and she had overheard her talking about her husband's new job.

No one, I imagine, is immune to politics of one kind or another. I have already told you how *Star* politics resulted in the killing of a couple of my stories. And company politics had a lot to do with my being allowed to remain a broadcaster at CFRB, and they were also the reason why I left the station. At the *Star*, there were two or three attempts to get me off the air, one of them by the great newspaperman Ralph Allen. He suggested to Beland Honderich that I should only be broadcasting news from the previous day. We had a meeting and I said, first of all, CFRB doesn't want stale news, and second, I don't want to be the guy giving day-old news over the air. If that's the case, I'll give it up. But Honderich put a stop to that scheme. I think he realized the *Star* was getting a certain amount of free advertising from my broadcasts. Also, Mrs. Hindmarsh, the daughter of the *Star*'s founder and widow of Harry C. Hindmarsh, loved to hear my reports, and I think some of the higher-ups knew this.

Thus, I stayed at CFRB for twenty-five years, signing off each broadcast with the words, "This is Jocko Thomas from po-lice headquarrrters," growling out the last word, which had begun as a bit of fun on my part and soon became my signature. New management took over CFRB in 1985, and in November of that year they had a party to celebrate my twenty-fifth anniversary at the station. But things were changing. Early in 1986, the news director informed me that it had come to his attention that I didn't know how to pronounce the words "police headquarters" and asked me to correct that fault. The few times I tried, people thought I must be ill. Then, in March, the news director took me to lunch and said that from now on, I had to keep my broadcasts down to twenty-five seconds. It was then that I realized what was going on: they were thinking in terms of a new format and a new style and wanted me to leave without their actually having to fire me. This didn't hurt or annoy me; the job had never been that lucrative, and I'd been at it for a long time. I went home and wrote my resignation.

Two days later, when I was sure the station had got the letter, I called the *Star*, thinking my resignation would make a nice little item for the radio column. The city editor put the rewrite man on to me. I told him the story, including the part about not being able to pronounce police headquarters. That made the headline. I'd had no intention of embarrassing the station, but when the story came out in the paper they were inundated with letters and calls from surprised listeners. I was also interviewed on radio and TV, and the radio commentators especially leapt on the opportunity to ridicule CFRB. As a result, someone from the station called and asked me to come back. I said I'd stand by my resignation. "We won't accept it," he said. "I don't care if you accept it or not," I replied. "It's done. That's it." Other stations offered me jobs, but I turned them down, too. I'd had enough of radio. And anyway, I was still a newspaper reporter, which was all I had ever wanted to be.

27

Dead Children

OVER A PERIOD OF NINE MONTHS, from about mid-1980 to March 1981, someone played God in the cardiac ward at Toronto's Hospital for Sick Children and decided that twenty-three babies should die. The case has been covered extensively by all the media, and I am not going to re-hash it here. All I want to do is point out a few facts.

The primary one is that a killer got away with twenty-three murders right under the eyes of all the authorities: hospital, police and the courts. When the preliminary hearing quite rightly dismissed the charges against nurse Susan Nelles, this was seen as proof of how well our justice system works. The fact of the matter is that except for the preliminary hearing procedure, *no part* of the system worked at all well, starting with the hospital.

The series of highly unusual deaths in the cardiac ward was common knowledge at the hospital. The nurses concerned were even attending counseling sessions to help them cope with the tragedies, but the police were not alerted until the very end, and even then it was not the hospital that sounded the alarm. It was the coroner, Paul Tepperman. The police then came under enormous pressure to solve the case quickly. Jack Press and Tony Warr, the two homicide sergeants who were assigned to it, had no particular medical or hospital expertise. It just happened to be their weekend to work when the call came through. They began their investigation on March 22, 1981, and Susan Nelles was charged three days later. The basis of the case against her was her connection with one of the dead babies; her access to the digoxin that was used to kill the children; and the fact that she said she wanted a lawyer present when she talked to the police, which she had a perfect right to do.

To my mind, if the police had not acted so hastily, they could have caught the killer red-handed, or at the very least built up a strong case. There are female police officers who have trained as nurses. Undercover operations are an almost routine part of police work. So why was a policewoman not integrated into the ward's nursing staff to see what was really going on? Everyone concerned with the investigation, including the homicide team, seemed to feel that haste was necessary. And to be fair, their concern was well founded. While the coroner and hospital heads were investigating the fatal dose of digoxin given to one baby, another baby, who shouldn't have had any digoxin in his system at all, was given a lethal dose of it. Thus, a prolonged investigation might have meant the sacrifice of more babies. That must have weighed heavily on the authorities' minds. But the haste with which the inquiry was pursued led only to a monumental bungle and the killer going free.

As wrong as they were, the police and the Crown attorney truly believed the evidence did point to Susan Nelles. I didn't cover the preliminary hearing. That was done by Virginia Corner. There was a ban on the publication of any testimony, but Virginia went to the court every day and wrote up the proceedings just as if they were to run in the paper. She did that so we would have an account of the hearing and be ready for the trial. But all of a sudden, it didn't look as if there would *be* a trial. The word around the newsroom was, "You hear what's going *on* over there? They got the wrong woman. The evidence is pointing to another nurse." When I mentioned this to the brass at headquarters, they still seemed to believe there was no chance of any other result than a committal for trial. Bob McGee, the Crown counsel, felt the same. He argued right to the end for Nelles to go before a Supreme Court jury, but Judge David Vanek discharged her.

A royal commission was ordered to look into the babies' deaths in December 1984, but its scope was stunted by an appeal court ruling that it could not assign criminal blame for the slayings, nor could it place civil responsibility. I have never understood that. The ruling made Mr. Justice Samuel Grange's royal commission unlike any other I have ever covered. For example, the royal commission into the operations of the Hundred Percent Gang, which I mentioned near the beginning of the book, not only resulted in criminal charges being laid against many policemen. It also broadened into an inquiry into other aspects of police management and linked some top brass with unsavory characters. Similarly, the royal commission that followed the Dorland affair came right out and said some police brass were liars and ordered that one detective be charged with shooting with intent to kill or maim. I could cite many other examples. But the Grange Royal Commission had no power and ended up only confirming what everyone already knew: twenty-three babies were murdered.

After Grange returned his report, the Metro police commission said the $250,000 reward for information leading to the arrest and conviction of the killer still stood. The public was assured that the case was still open, and technically it still is now, but the killer is never going to stand trial unless she comes forward and confesses.

Mr. Justice Grange was compassionate, in that he didn't blame anyone or even hint that anyone was to blame for the failure to solve the baby murders. But the case was the worst thing that had ever happened to the Metro force, and heads had to roll. There was no immediate shake-up, but little by little changes were made. Sergeant Tony Warr, who had just joined the homicide squad and had been on his first murder investigation, was the first to leave. He took a job with the Ontario Fire Marshal's office. However, he did return quietly to the force in May 1990, though at a lower rank, and is now doing divisional detective work. Jack Press was transferred from the homicide squad to the internal trial office, which prepares evidence for the court martial-style hearings of officers charged under the Police Act. Press is now executive assistant to Dr. John Hillsdon-Smith, Ontario's chief pathologist.

Bob Bamlett, the chief of detectives, and Jim Crawford, the head of the homicide squad, were also moved to other jobs. Bamlett resigned on pension soon afterward. Crawford, an excellent detective, who had worked on some two hundred murder cases in almost fifteen years, was placed in charge of the criminal investigation branch in North York. To insiders on the force, he and Bamlett were simply scapegoats. Their transfers certainly did nothing to change the fact that the murderer of twenty-three babies is still at large.

Throughout this book, I have mentioned how much I enjoyed my job, but I must now qualify that. With the exception of the Peter Woodcock case, I have said next to nothing about the murders of children, which were always dreadful things to cover. In far too many cases, the killer is a fiend (there is no other word) and reporters rarely even hint at the hideous and sickening details that emerge in the homicide and autopsy reports. These tell stories that are almost too horrid to contemplate and make you want to push the terrible truth that human beings are capable of such atrocities out of your mind. But you can't. The horror stays with you forever, down to the smallest detail.

Such atrocities are not a modern phenomenon. I could recite a litany of children's names that goes back to the very beginning of my career. Judy Carter, Emanuel Jaques, Lynne Harper, Linda Lampkin, Patricia Lipton, Allison Parrott and Tristan Jaime Shearer are only a few of the many victims I could cite. These children haunt me. Each died a terrible death, but the one that hit me the hardest, shook me as badly as I was shaken the day I sat in the courtroom and heard Arthur Kendall's children describing the cold-blooded slaughter of their mother, was the murder of Tristan Shearer. He died not because he had excited the lust of some pervert, but simply because his presence on this earth had become inconvenient.

Tristan was a pleasant, curly-haired little boy with a fantastic memory. His superior intelligence was quickly recognized by the staff at the Vancouver kindergarten where his mother, Maureen Christiansen Shearer, enrolled him. Tristan was five and Maureen was twenty-six. She was divorced from Tristan's father and studying anthropology at the University of British Columbia. Sometime around 1975, while spending an afternoon in a local park, Maureen and the boy were approached by a smooth-talking man who regaled them with tales of his glamorous life in Florida. This was Ray Carter, thirty-five, an escapee from Raiford Penitentiary, where he had been serving a life sentence for murder. His lies enthralled Maureen, and she and Carter were soon married. He pretended to be fond of Tristan, who quickly became attached to him, readily accepting Ray and Maureen's contention that this man was now his father. When Carter eventually disclosed his true past to Maureen, it did nothing to diminish her great love for him.

In the summer of 1976, Ray, Maureen and Tristan moved to Toronto, where Carter began acquiring credit cards under various false names. He and Maureen also registered for welfare under several assumed names and got it. What they couldn't get was a furnished flat. The landlords they approached didn't want children in their buildings. So Carter convinced Maureen that the only thing to do was kill Tristan. Totally in thrall of her husband to begin with, Maureen was also a bit of a mystic, believing that if the spirit is strong enough, a person can die and return to life. She and Carter began telling Tristan about this, saying they were all going to die, and that he would probably be the first to go, but they would all come back and live out west in a cabin in the mountains.

Toward the end of July 1976, after having been turned down by another landlord and living for a time in an emergency housing facility, Carter drove to Springwater Provincial Park with Maureen, Tristan and a Siamese cat that Maureen had acquired. Just before they reached the park, which is near Barrie, about fifty miles north of Toronto, they had Tristan hide under a blanket in the back of the car so the gate attendant wouldn't see him. Then, when Carter had found what looked like a suitable spot, they stopped and spread the blanket on the ground. And while Maureen sat on it, sunning herself and playing with the cat, Carter took Tristan into the woods and strangled him.

Now another element enters the story, giving it an even more macabre twist. Tristan's bones were found the following April. Previous to that, John Rallo, a former OPP officer and manager of Hamilton City Hall, had murdered his wife and two young children. The mother and daughter were found in Lake Ontario, off St. Catharines. The hunt went on for the boy, Jason. When Tristan's remains were discovered, it seemed odd, what with the other two bodies having been found in the water, but it was assumed that Rallo had for some reason disposed of his son's body in Springwater Park. Thus, Tristan was buried as Jason in Mrs. Rallo's family's plot in Hamilton.

Meanwhile, after staying for a time in a flat in Toronto, Ray and Maureen moved to Edmonton, where her family lived. To her parents' increasingly anxious inquiries about their grandson, Maureen vaguely said something about him staying with friends in Toronto. She and Carter, who had been living on his fraudulent credit cards, eventually took jobs as maintenance employees at a supermarket in Grande-Prairie, Alberta. A couple of months later, Carter removed $5,000 from the store's safe, and they fled to Hope, B.C., where the RCMP caught up with them and returned the couple to Grande-Prairie. This was now the spring of 1977.

Carter then did what psychotic criminals often do. He started blabbing. He told the RCMP that he had helped a man who had killed his wife and daughter dispose of a body near the entrance to a provincial park in Ontario. He would, he said, give them more details if the supermarket charge against his wife was dropped and he was not charged as an accessory to the Ontario murder.

The RCMP asked the OPP to check the story out, and the task fell to Inspector Casey Kotwa. As far as he could see, the only murder that fit the one Carter had described was the killing of Jason Rallo. Meanwhile, Carter and Maureen were released from custody, pending trial for the supermarket job.

On May 13, they made a suicide pact and tried to strangle each other. They failed and were taken to a psychiatric hospital in Edmonton. Three weeks later, Carter confessed to the slaying of Tristan Jaime Shearer.

Back in Ontario, Inspector Kotwa placed the facts before Ontario's chief coroner, W. B. Cotnam, and got permission to exhume Jason/Tristan's body from the grave in Hamilton. The boy's teeth were compared with charts obtained from a Vancouver dentist, and the body was finally identified as Tristan's. Kotwa then went out to Edmonton with Constable Ed Ziliotto, and they tape-recorded Carter's rambling, almost nonchalant confession. As he told how he had taken Tristan into the woods to see the birds and strangled him, there was not a break in his voice or any other sign of remorse.

Kotwa and Ziliotto then went to the park with Carter, and he walked them to the exact spot where the boy's remains had been found. Back in Edmonton sometime later, Kotwa arranged to see Maureen at the house of a relative, where she was staying. The next day, shortly before the appointed time, Maureen put the muzzle of a shotgun into her mouth and pulled the trigger.

Ray Carter was sentenced to life in prison for second degree murder. Somewhere along the line, he was sent to a penitentiary near Drumheller, Alberta. In January 1990, while I was preparing this book, I saw in the paper that he had escaped while working outside the prison on a pass.

I may be out of the running now, but the race goes on.

28

So Long

ON MARCH 3, 1989, after sixty years and forty-three city editors, I retired from the *Toronto Star*. I have to admit that I still miss being part of the hustle and excitement of putting out the paper every day. Preparing these memoirs has been a help, but I still haven't shaken that lost and empty feeling. I suppose it will wear off, eventually. At least I *hope* it does.

Shortly after I retired, I received two special honors from the police community. The first was an honorary membership, complete with an authentic gold badge, in the Metropolitan Toronto Police Association, which is the police union. The second was from the Metropolitan Toronto Police Pensioners' Association, which surprised me by making me an honorary member, too. It was at one of their regular meetings, and I was called upon to make a short speech. Looking into the crowd, I spotted Humphrey Hewitt sitting there, so I told the gathering about the day I wrote his obituary, almost forty-five years ago.

Humphrey and I and his brother-in-law, a very able sergeant of detectives named John Hicks, used to go to the Long Branch horse races on our days off. Although she never bet, John's wife, Sarah, used to go, too, and I remember one terribly rainy day when she said we should put our money on a horse called Lace Shawl, because she liked the name and she liked the look of the beast. Of course, being meticulous, scientific bettors we ignored her hunch, and

Lace Shawl paid eighty dollars. That sort of thing tends to stick in a horse player's mind. But I also remember the day because the next time I saw Humphrey, he was in a hospital emergency ward. The doctors and nurses were shaking their heads and policemen were dashing in to ask if he was still alive.

That Sunday morning, Humphrey had been given the job of riding in the back of a patrol wagon that was taking a group of prisoners from a downtown police station to the jail. It was considered necessary to have a cop in the back because the drunks had been known to turn on one another with near-fatal results during the short trip. This time, however, someone had not searched them properly, and one of the prisoners pulled out a pistol and put several bullets into Humphrey's stomach and chest. But he didn't get away. Humphrey still had enough strength to grab the guy's leg and hold him till the driver stopped the wagon and came to his aid. After seeing him at the hospital, I went to the office and wrote Humphrey's obituary in advance. As I told the pensioners that night, I didn't think he would live out the week. But there he was at the meeting, badly bent with arthritis, but still as jovial at the age of ninety-two as he was when he patrolled the downtown beats.

When it came time to see who was the oldest person at the meeting, Humphrey waved his cane, but he didn't get the door prize. It was won by man of ninety-three. "Maybe I'll make it next year," Humphrey said, "but I hope I don't, because that'll mean that other poor devil will have to die."

Old police officers aren't like old reporters, who hang around the bars at press clubs, rehashing their scoops and swapping stories. Old cops hardly ever talk about their cases, but they do tend to keep in touch with one another. This is because policemen stay together always. When they are on the force, the very nature of their work means they can't socialize with a lot of other people, and this carries on into their retirement.

That meeting where I was made an honorary member of the association was by no means the first I had been to. I have always enjoyed their gatherings, because I invariably run into many of the people that I spent my professional life with. More than a few were friends as well as contacts. To name only three that come to mind, there was George Laird, a kindly, Irish-born former sergeant who lived until he was ninety and led the fight to get a better deal for the police pensioners. The police who retire today get a pretty good deal, but there was a time not long ago when cops who'd retired on pensions of $800 and $1,000 a year were being impoverished by inflation.

There was also Joe Shield, a former detective, who had a tooth shot out one night as he was chasing a gunman down an alley. Joe got the King's Medal and brand-new gold tooth.

The third name that comes to mind is Paddy Hogan, who dated from the days when the Orange Order controlled city hall. There were twelve divisional inspectors on the force then, one of them being the token Roman Catholic. When Paddy was promoted to this post, I heard it at a police commission meeting and called him for an interview. The trouble was, no one had yet told him about his promotion, so I didn't get the interview because whenever he stopped laughing at the idea, all he would say was, "You can't fool me, Tufty. You can't fool me." He thought I was Sergeant Tuft, the resident practical joker at headquarters.

What I'm saying here is that at these police pensioners meetings I meet a tremendous number of people from my own past, many of them going back to the days when it was almost possible to know everyone on the force. I also see a lot of the city's history in these men and women. Moreover, when I got older and went on working past the normal retirement age, I also began to see people who had started on the police force long after I had become a reporter, worked out their entire careers and retired. These people often thought it odd that I was still working, and a few years ago, one of them asked why I had not retired, as well. "Someone has to stay around and write your obituaries," I said. Everyone laughed. But I meant it. And I still do.

Index

Adair, Dave, 101
Adamson, Harold, 143, 193, 198-200
Allen, Ralph, 202
Amiel, Barbara, 140
Anderson, Charlie, 182-84
Appleby, Lou, 34
Armstrong, Barney, 51-52
Atkinson, Joseph E.
  new building, 10
  "Red *Star*," 37, 64
  and staff, 12, 13, 26
  versus gambling, 54
  death, 151
Atkinson, Joseph S., 163, 178

Baker, Alden, 170
Ballard, Harold, 196-97
Bamlett, Bob, 191-93, 207
Bannon, James, 32
Barlow, Fred, 83, 92, 94, 96-97, 99
Barrie, Ronald, 100-103
Bartlett, Jimmy, 27, 179-80
Bassett, John, 62, 146, 157-58
Beasley, Bill, 53
Belland, Lee, 135-36, 138-39
Bell, Marilyn, 156-59
Berkley, Herb, 30-31
Bick, Charles O. (Bob)
  appointment, 166-67
  and James Mackey, 174-75
  and John Chisholm, 169, 171-73
  and John Murray, 194
  and Lastman "kidnapping," 198
  politics of office, 166-67, 196, 200-202
  resigns, 200-202
Blackwell, Leslie, 83, 107
Blanchard, Doug, 31
Bluestein, Max, 176

Bohozuk, William, 89-92, 98-99
Bolton, Bill, 129, 168
Booth, Jack, 117
Borins, Norman, 106
Boyd, Doreen, 126-27, 129
Boyd, Edwin Alonzo, 121-23, 126-28, 130-32
Boyd Gang, 2, 121-32, 160
Boyd, John, 24
Boyd, Norman, 123, 126-27
Bracebridge, Ontario, 102
Breathalyzer scam, 190-93
Brickell, Norm, 146
Bridle, Augustus, 11
Brown, Playfair, 51
Bryant, George, 157, 159
Buckowski, Jean, 111, 112-13
Buckowski, Stanley, 110-20
Bull (Colonel), 69
Bull, Henry, 161
Bull, W. Perkins, 24
Burnett, Red, 11-13
Burton, C. L., 43-44

Callwood, June, 158
Cameron, Ross, 182
Carter, Ray, 208-10
Carty, Arthur, 29
Casnig, Bernice, 82, 85-86
censorship, 67, 69-70, 80
Chadwick, Florence, 156-57
Checkley, Harry, 42-45
Cherry Nose (police officer), 25-26, 79-80
child molesting, 14-15, 59
Chisholm, John, 164-74
  chief of detectives, 30, 39, 164-65
  police chief, 33, 87, 111, 127, 165-73
  and politicians, 165-67, 178

and press, 62, 80, 169, 172
suicide, 2, 172-73
Cobourg, Ontario, 72-78
Cochrane, Ontario, 104-5
Cole, Art, 101
Cole, Cyril, 191-93
Cole, Percy, 31, 69
Conacher, Lionel, 54
Conboy, Fred, 79
Constable, Tommy, 169, 171-72
Corner, Virginia, 205
Cotnam, W. B., 210
court reporting, 11, 13-15, 17-20
Craft, Austin, 105-8
Craven, Ken, 126-27
Crawford, Jim, 161, 207
Creighton, Lloyd, 197
Cronk, Doug, 115-16
Cunningham, William Wallace, 73-75, 77-78
Currie, Donald, 185

Davey, Scotty, 51
Davies, Major, 18
Davies, Stan, 95
Davis, Fred, 74-76, 84-86
Davis, Grenville, 178
death penalty, 48
Dick, Evelyn, 87-99, 101, 104
Dick, John, 88-95, 98
Dinino, Margaret Currie, 185-88
Dinino, Stephenino, 185-89
Dinsmore, Ted, 157
Domm, Gordon, 54
Dorland, Albert, 37-38, 206
Draper, Dennis C., 33-39
    appointment, 33-35
    and convicts, 40, 59
    murder cases, 34, 59
    police corruption, 52
    political connections, 34-35, 37-39
    and press, 30, 35-37, 52, 59
    on trial, 72-73
    war effort, 79
    retires as chief, 87-88
Drylie, John, 15, 29
Dubin, Charles, 152
Dunn, Eddie, 167-68

Earl, Marjorie, 92-94
Egan, Fred, 30-31
Etobicoke torture scandal, 168, 190
executions. See also hangings
    firing squad, 120
    gas chamber, 2, 110, 119
    public interest, 47, 85
    reporters as witnesses, 1-2, 47, 118
    U.S. committee, 110, 119-20

Fabian (Inspector), 145-48

Fardella, Agnes, 73-77
Fardella, Tony, 76
Feder, Manny, 51, 53, 55
Feely (gambler), 179
female reporters, 13
Forsythe, Robert, 135-36, 138
Fort Frances, Ontario, 1, 82-85
Fort William, Ontario, 149-51, 153, 155
Franks, Wilford, 104
fraud, 196-97
Frost, Leslie, 129, 152, 166, 179

Gale, Jack, 157
Gallo, Louis, 61
gambling, 27, 50-56, 57-60, 176-79
Gandier, Donald, 151-53
Garcia, Aurelio, 186-87
Gardiner, Fred (Big Daddy), 165-66, 170-71
Garner, Hugh, 11-12
Garrity, Dave, 53
Garson, Stuart, 153
Gault, Howard Ferguson, 122
Gauthier, Roger, 104-5
German Canadians, interned, 67
German POWs, 67-71
Gibb, Alexandrine, 4, 13, 17, 173
Gibson, Dick, 161
Gill, Ernie, 200
Gillespie, Jack, 126, 129
Givens, Phil, 195, 201-2
Goodman, Eddie, 201
Goodman, Martin, 190-93, 195
Gouzenko, Igor, 134-41
Gouzenko (Mrs.), 140-41
Gow, Athol
    as author's senior, 20, 23, 52
    and Dennis Draper, 35-37
    ghostwriting for Red Ryan, 40-41
    retires, 87, 98
Graham, Harold, 146, 181-83
Grange, Samuel, 206
Gravenhurst, Ontario, 68-69
Greenaway, Roy, 40-41, 52, 74-75, 77, 166
Griffin, Dave, 59-61
Guthrie, George, 40

Hamilton, Ontario, 60-61, 88-89, 91-92, 98
hangings. See also executions
    Austin Craft, 106-8
    Hot Stove murderers, 1, 82-86
    Lennie Jackson, 131-32
    for killing prison guard, 2
    Harry O'Donnell, 45-47
    Popoviches, 2, 108
    reporters as witnesses, 47
    Steve Suchan, 131-32
Harper, Lynne, 184
Hartt, Patrick, 162
Heron, John R., 29

Hewitt, Humphrey, 211-12
Hibbs, Sid, 28-29, 61
Hicks, John, 211
Hicks, Sarah, 211
Highways Department scandal, 149-54
Hillsdon-Smith, John, 207
Hindmarsh, Harry A., 152, 156
Hindmarsh, Harry C.
    and author's libel suit, 140
    Boyd Gang, 129
    Buckowski execution, 115, 118
    Fardella case, 74
    legendary, 10, 76
Hindmarsh, John, 10, 26
Hindmarsh (Mrs. Harry C.), 202
Hogan, Pat, 42-43, 213
Hogue, Beatrice, 181, 183-84
holdups
    banks, 37-38, 63, 122-23
    common during Depression, 23
    Dorland case, 37-38
    Etobicoke torture scandal, 168
    pharmacies, 80-81
    Red Ryan, 41
Honderich, Beland, 141, 202
Hope, Clare, 102-3
Horlick (Mrs.), 24
Hot Stove case, 1, 82-86
Howarth, Dorothy, 157
Hughes, Elwood, 4
Human Target case, 48-49
Hundred Percent Gang, 25-26, 206
Huntsville, Ontario, 70-71

Italian Canadians, interned, 67

Jackson, Anne, 126, 129
Jackson, Lennie, 121, 123-32
Jackson, William (Willie the Clown), 121,
    123, 127-28, 130
Jamieson, Viola, 82-83, 85
Johnstone, Walter, 175
Jukes, Harold, 126

Keay, Art, 89-90
Keith, William, 14-15
Kelly, Frank, 82-83, 131
Kendall, Anne, 182-84
Kendall, Arthur, 181-84
Kendall, Helen, 181-84
Kendall, Jimmy, 182-84
Kendall, Margaret, 182-84
Kennedy, John, 105-6
Kent, Palmer, 39
Kettlewell, Christina, 100-104
Kettlewell, Jack, 100-103
kidnapping, 26, 28-32, 142-44, 146, 197-200
Kingsbury, Jim, 74
Kingsley, W. T., 40, 43

Kingstone (judge), 38
Kingston, Ontario, 2, 107
Knowles, Russell, 32
Knowles, Vernon, 26-27
Kotwa, Casey, 209-10

Labatt, Hugh, 30-31
Labatt, John Sackville, 28, 29-30, 32
Laird, George, 213
Lamport, Allan, 127, 135, 158
Lastman, Marilyn, 197-200
Lastman, Mel, 197-200
Lauzon, Ulysses, 63
Lawson, Smirle, 83
Layng, Arthur, 111-12, 114, 116-17
libel suit against author, 134, 136-40
Lott, Peter, 192-93
Loudon, Julian, 34
Lytle, Tommy, 104, 150-51

McCardell, Michael, 29, 32
McCathie, Archie, 38
McClellan, George, 136
McClement, Fred, 101
McCulloch, Harvey, 94
McDermott (gambler), 179
MacDonald, Alex, 61-62
MacDonald, Edwin, 63
MacDonald, Kitty Kat, 62
MacDonald, Mickey, 61-63
McDowell, Marion, 142-48, 166
McGee, Bob, 205
McGill, Garnet, 179
McKay, Gloria, 114, 117-18
McKay, Robert, 114, 117-18
Mackey, James, 172, 174-76, 178, 193, 198
MacLean, Alexandra, 88-90, 97
MacLean, Donald, 88, 90-92, 98
McLean, J. S., 26, 32
McMullen, Ed (Wyoming), 42-43
MacPherson, Duncan, 141
McRuer, James C., 39, 131, 162-63
Mafia, 60, 175-76
Maloney, Arthur, 131
Marsh, Lou, 4, 51
Martin, Goldwyn Arthur, 63, 98-99, 160
Meisner, David, 32
Milne, Gib, 74, 77-78
Minelli, Nick, 63
Montreal, Quebec, 125-26
Moore, C. Frank, 15
Morgan, Jim, 198
murders
    author's first report, 20-21
    gangland. See murder victims, Jimmy
        Windsor
    Hospital for Sick Children, 204-7
    Hot Stove case. See murder victims,
        Viola Jamieson

Human Target case, 48
multiple, 2, 48, 113-14, 116-18
murder victims
Lou Appleby, 34
bootlegger, 108
children, 89-91, 98, 160-61, 184, 204-10
William Wallace Cunningham, 73-78
John Dick, 88-95, 98
Margaret Dinino, 185-88
Agnes Fardella, 73-78
Viola Jamieson, 1, 82-85
Helen Kendall, 181-84
Christina Kettlewell, 100-104
Arthur Layng, 111-12, 114, 116-17
Marion McDowell, 142-48
McKay couple, 114, 117-18
police officers, 2, 41, 43, 124-25, 127, 129
prison guard, 2
Stouffville car dealer, 42
Tristan Shearer, 207-10
Ruth Taylor, 45-48
Valair Vandebelt, 104-5
Peter David White, 98
Jimmy Windsor, 57-61
Murphy, Eddie, 73
Murray (chief of detectives), 38
Murray, John, 192-95

Napanee, Ontario, 48
National Newspaper Award, 118, 140, 149, 195
Nelles, Susan, 204-5
Nimmo, John, 69, 125, 160
North Bay, Ontario, 154-55

O'Donnell, Harry, 45-49
O'Donnell (Mrs.), 46-47
Oliver, Charlie, 22, 23-24, 26, 171
Oliver, Doug, 47-48
Olsen, Bob, 141
Orillia, Ontario, 101
Orpen, Abe, 53, 55
Ouellette, Andy, 129-31

Papalia, Johnny, 176
Parry Sound, Ontario, 65
Pascoe, Claud, 30, 47-48
Patterson, Margaret, 17-18
Payne, Adolphus
Boyd Gang, 122-23, 126-27, 132
Buckowski case, 112, 114
Lastman "kidnapping," 199-200
"Trigger," 22
peeper, 79-80
Perez, Sabina, 185-87
Perri, Bessie, 60
Perri, Rocco, 60
Perry, Roy, 124-26, 130

Phelan, Thomas N., 137-39
Philby, Kim, 135
Phillips, Norman, 70-71
Pinky (bagman), 51
police
and politics, 166-67, 176-80, 196-203
relationship with press, 22-25, 35-37, 59, 60-62, 80-81, 169
police corruption, 25-27, 51-52, 168, 178-79, 190-95
police officers, murdered, 2, 41, 43, 124-25, 127, 129
Popovich, Elizabeth, 2, 108
Popovich, George, 2, 108
Porter, Dana, 146, 148
Poulton, Ron, 110, 118-19
Powell, Clay, 197
Press, Jack, 204, 206
Preston, Clarence, 89, 91-95, 98
Price, William H., 38

Rallo, Jason, 209-10
Rallo, John, 209
Rasky, Harry, 130
Regan, Frank, 46-48, 62
Richardson, Maurice, 130
Rigney, Timothy, 92, 94
Roach, Wilfred, 179
robbery. See holdups
Roberts, Kelso, 179
Robinette, John J., 97-98, 105, 131
Robinson, W. L., 83
Roebuck, Arthur, 47-48
Rogers, L. Joslyn, 45
Rose, Fred, 134
Royal Tour of 1939, 64-65
Ryan, Norman (Red), 40-43
Ryder, Gus, 156-57, 159

Samuel, Ian, 191-92, 194-95
San Francisco, California, 110, 119
Sarnia, Ontario, 41-43
Saunders, Bob, 87
Sayeau, Harry, 183
Scanlon, Joe, 168
Schmidt, William, 82-86
Schreiber, Norma, 145
Sedgwick, Joe, 84
Sellar, George, 161
Sharpe, Noble, 147
Shea, John, 61-63
Shearer, Maureen Christiansen, 208-10
Shearer, Tristan Jaime, 207-10
Shepherd, Sam, 148
Shield, Joe, 213
Shulman, Morton, 160-61, 192
Silk, Eric, 179, 181
Simmonds, Bernard, 131, 199-200
Sinclair, Gordon, 11, 68, 129, 152, 199-200

Sisco, Rocco, 104-5
Skrypnyk, Anthony, 82-84, 86
Skrypnyk, George, 82-84, 86
Smith, Paul, 145, 150
Smith, Strathy, 68, 70-71
Smythe, Stafford, 196-97
Snyder, Cecil L., 62-63, 83, 89-90
Spears, Borden, 115, 138, 150, 160, 161, 173
spies, 65-67, 134-41
Stanley, Art, 8-9
Stanley, Marjorie. See Thomas, Marjorie
Stark, Alexander, 137, 139
Star. See Toronto Star
Stewart, William, 38-39
Storm, Fred, 34
Suchan, Steve, 123-28, 130-32
Sullivan, John, 92-94

Tate, Alf, 92, 115
Taylor, Ruth, 45-48
Teets, Hartley, 118-19
Telford, Elizabeth, 108
Tepperman, Paul, 204
Teskey, Frank, 92, 104, 115
Teskey, Helen, 115
Thomas, Dave, 6
Thomas, Gregor, 6, 8
Thomas, Jocko
   childhood, 6-8
   parents, 5-8
   copy boy, 4-6, 8-15
   cub reporter, 16-27
   reporter, 28-86
   senior reporter, 87-210
   libel suit, 134, 136-40
   wins National Newspaper Award, 118, 140, 149, 195
   radio reporter, 140, 163, 202-3
   retirement, 211-13
Thomas, Marjorie, 19, 44, 64, 124, 160
Thomas, Ron, 44, 64, 124, 159-60
Thompson, Bill, 126
Three-fingered Abe. See McCardell, Michael
Thurston, Herb, 175-76
Tijuana, Mexico, 185-88

Tilley, A. C. Alcot, 154
Tillonen, Eino, 82-84
Timson, Ray, 141
Tong, Edmund, 124-27, 129-30
Toohey (informer), 37-38
Toronto Star
   building, 10
   female reporters, 13
   and the government, 149-55
   newsroom, 10-11
   procedures, 10-13, 19
   single copy, 46-47
Trotter, Bert, 130
Truscott, Steven, 183-84
Tuft (Sergeant), 213
Turner, John, 197
Turofsky, Nat, 5
Twaddle (Constable), 183

Urquhart, Howard, 105-6

Van, Arthur, 55
Vandebelt, Valair, 104-5
Vanek, David, 205

Walkerton, Ontario, 184
Ward, Albert, 82-83
Ward, Paddy, 7
Warr, Tony, 204, 206
wartime, and the press, 64-65
Welland, Ontario, 2, 108
Wemp, Bert, 39, 69
White, Peter David, 98
Wiarton, Ontario, 181-82
Wilson, Jimmy, 142-44, 147
Windsor, Jimmy, 57-61
Wintermeyer, John, 179
women reporters. See female reporters
Wood, Charlie, 89, 91-95, 98
Woodcock, Peter, 160-63
Worthington, Peter, 140
Wright, Tom, 101

Young, George, 4-5
Young, Roly, 16

Ziliotto, Ed, 210